C-136 CAREER EXAMINATION SERIES

This is your
PASSBOOK for...

Civil Engineer

Test Preparation Study Guide
Questions & Answers

NATIONAL LEARNING CORPORATION®

COPYRIGHT NOTICE

This book is SOLELY intended for, is sold ONLY to, and its use is RESTRICTED to individual, bona fide applicants or candidates who qualify by virtue of having seriously filed applications for appropriate license, certificate, professional and/or promotional advancement, higher school matriculation, scholarship, or other legitimate requirements of education and/or governmental authorities.

This book is NOT intended for use, class instruction, tutoring, training, duplication, copying, reprinting, excerption, or adaptation, etc., by:

1) Other publishers
2) Proprietors and/or Instructors of "Coaching" and/or Preparatory Courses
3) Personnel and/or Training Divisions of commercial, industrial, and governmental organizations
4) Schools, colleges, or universities and/or their departments and staffs, including teachers and other personnel
5) Testing Agencies or Bureaus
6) Study groups which seek by the purchase of a single volume to copy and/or duplicate and/or adapt this material for use by the group as a whole without having purchased individual volumes for each of the members of the group
7) Et al.

Such persons would be in violation of appropriate Federal and State statutes.

PROVISION OF LICENSING AGREEMENTS – Recognized educational, commercial, industrial, and governmental institutions and organizations, and others legitimately engaged in educational pursuits, including training, testing, and measurement activities, may address request for a licensing agreement to the copyright owners, who will determine whether, and under what conditions, including fees and charges, the materials in this book may be used them. In other words, a licensing facility exists for the legitimate use of the material in this book on other than an individual basis. However, it is asseverated and affirmed here that the material in this book CANNOT be used without the receipt of the express permission of such a licensing agreement from the Publishers. Inquiries re licensing should be addressed to the company, attention rights and permissions department.

All rights reserved, including the right of reproduction in whole or in part, in any form or by any means, electronic or mechanical, including photocopying, recording, or by any information storage and retrieval system, without permission in writing from the Publisher.

Copyright © 2024 by
National Learning Corporation

212 Michael Drive, Syosset, NY 11791
(516) 921-8888 • www.passbooks.com
E-mail: info@passbooks.com

PUBLISHED IN THE UNITED STATES OF AMERICA

PASSBOOK® SERIES

THE *PASSBOOK® SERIES* has been created to prepare applicants and candidates for the ultimate academic battlefield – the examination room.

At some time in our lives, each and every one of us may be required to take an examination – for validation, matriculation, admission, qualification, registration, certification, or licensure.

Based on the assumption that every applicant or candidate has met the basic formal educational standards, has taken the required number of courses, and read the necessary texts, the *PASSBOOK® SERIES* furnishes the one special preparation which may assure passing with confidence, instead of failing with insecurity. Examination questions – together with answers – are furnished as the basic vehicle for study so that the mysteries of the examination and its compounding difficulties may be eliminated or diminished by a sure method.

This book is meant to help you pass your examination provided that you qualify and are serious in your objective.

The entire field is reviewed through the huge store of content information which is succinctly presented through a provocative and challenging approach – the question-and-answer method.

A climate of success is established by furnishing the correct answers at the end of each test.

You soon learn to recognize types of questions, forms of questions, and patterns of questioning. You may even begin to anticipate expected outcomes.

You perceive that many questions are repeated or adapted so that you can gain acute insights, which may enable you to score many sure points.

You learn how to confront new questions, or types of questions, and to attack them confidently and work out the correct answers.

You note objectives and emphases, and recognize pitfalls and dangers, so that you may make positive educational adjustments.

Moreover, you are kept fully informed in relation to new concepts, methods, practices, and directions in the field.

You discover that you are actually taking the examination all the time: you are preparing for the examination by "taking" an examination, not by reading extraneous and/or supererogatory textbooks.

In short, this PASSBOOK®, used directedly, should be an important factor in helping you to pass your test.

CIVIL ENGINEER

DUTIES:
Performs professional engineering duties in connection with the design, construction, inspection or maintenance of public works projects such as highways, bridges and sewer projects. Makes preliminary layouts and final designs; prepares engineering estimates of quantities of materials needed and prepares or modifies specifications for materials. Acts as resident project engineer on construction under contract to various contractors. Supervises construction and inspection; prepares cost estimates; supervises the sampling and testing of construction materials. Reviews engineering plans for compliance with county, state and federal standards for design and construction. Performs related duties as required.

SCOPE OF THE EXAMINATION:
The written test will cover knowledge, skills, and/or abilities in such areas as:
1. Principles and practices of civil engineering;
2. Engineering plans, specifications and estimates;
3. Methods and materials of construction;
4. Construction and maintenance of highways, bridges, drainage systems and other related structures;
5. Planning, design and construction of sanitary sewers; and
6. Supervision.

HOW TO TAKE A TEST

I. YOU MUST PASS AN EXAMINATION

A. WHAT EVERY CANDIDATE SHOULD KNOW

Examination applicants often ask us for help in preparing for the written test. What can I study in advance? What kinds of questions will be asked? How will the test be given? How will the papers be graded?

As an applicant for a civil service examination, you may be wondering about some of these things. Our purpose here is to suggest effective methods of advance study and to describe civil service examinations.

Your chances for success on this examination can be increased if you know how to prepare. Those "pre-examination jitters" can be reduced if you know what to expect. You can even experience an adventure in good citizenship if you know why civil service exams are given.

B. WHY ARE CIVIL SERVICE EXAMINATIONS GIVEN?

Civil service examinations are important to you in two ways. As a citizen, you want public jobs filled by employees who know how to do their work. As a job seeker, you want a fair chance to compete for that job on an equal footing with other candidates. The best-known means of accomplishing this two-fold goal is the competitive examination.

Exams are widely publicized throughout the nation. They may be administered for jobs in federal, state, city, municipal, town or village governments or agencies.

Any citizen may apply, with some limitations, such as the age or residence of applicants. Your experience and education may be reviewed to see whether you meet the requirements for the particular examination. When these requirements exist, they are reasonable and applied consistently to all applicants. Thus, a competitive examination may cause you some uneasiness now, but it is your privilege and safeguard.

C. HOW ARE CIVIL SERVICE EXAMS DEVELOPED?

Examinations are carefully written by trained technicians who are specialists in the field known as "psychological measurement," in consultation with recognized authorities in the field of work that the test will cover. These experts recommend the subject matter areas or skills to be tested; only those knowledges or skills important to your success on the job are included. The most reliable books and source materials available are used as references. Together, the experts and technicians judge the difficulty level of the questions.

Test technicians know how to phrase questions so that the problem is clearly stated. Their ethics do not permit "trick" or "catch" questions. Questions may have been tried out on sample groups, or subjected to statistical analysis, to determine their usefulness.

Written tests are often used in combination with performance tests, ratings of training and experience, and oral interviews. All of these measures combine to form the best-known means of finding the right person for the right job.

II. HOW TO PASS THE WRITTEN TEST

A. NATURE OF THE EXAMINATION

To prepare intelligently for civil service examinations, you should know how they differ from school examinations you have taken. In school you were assigned certain definite pages to read or subjects to cover. The examination questions were quite detailed and usually emphasized memory. Civil service exams, on the other hand, try to discover your present ability to perform the duties of a position, plus your potentiality to learn these duties. In other words, a civil service exam attempts to predict how successful you will be. Questions cover such a broad area that they cannot be as minute and detailed as school exam questions.

In the public service similar kinds of work, or positions, are grouped together in one "class." This process is known as *position-classification*. All the positions in a class are paid according to the salary range for that class. One class title covers all of these positions, and they are all tested by the same examination.

B. FOUR BASIC STEPS

1) Study the announcement

How, then, can you know what subjects to study? Our best answer is: "Learn as much as possible about the class of positions for which you've applied." The exam will test the knowledge, skills and abilities needed to do the work.

Your most valuable source of information about the position you want is the official exam announcement. This announcement lists the training and experience qualifications. Check these standards and apply only if you come reasonably close to meeting them.

The brief description of the position in the examination announcement offers some clues to the subjects which will be tested. Think about the job itself. Review the duties in your mind. Can you perform them, or are there some in which you are rusty? Fill in the blank spots in your preparation.

Many jurisdictions preview the written test in the exam announcement by including a section called "Knowledge and Abilities Required," "Scope of the Examination," or some similar heading. Here you will find out specifically what fields will be tested.

2) Review your own background

Once you learn in general what the position is all about, and what you need to know to do the work, ask yourself which subjects you already know fairly well and which need improvement. You may wonder whether to concentrate on improving your strong areas or on building some background in your fields of weakness. When the announcement has specified "some knowledge" or "considerable knowledge," or has used adjectives like "beginning principles of..." or "advanced ... methods," you can get a clue as to the number and difficulty of questions to be asked in any given field. More questions, and hence broader coverage, would be included for those subjects which are more important in the work. Now weigh your strengths and weaknesses against the job requirements and prepare accordingly.

3) Determine the level of the position

Another way to tell how intensively you should prepare is to understand the level of the job for which you are applying. Is it the entering level? In other words, is this the position in which beginners in a field of work are hired? Or is it an intermediate or advanced level? Sometimes this is indicated by such words as "Junior" or "Senior" in the class title. Other jurisdictions use Roman numerals to designate the level – Clerk I, Clerk II, for example. The word "Supervisor" sometimes appears in the title. If the level is not indicated by the title, check the description of duties. Will you be working under very close supervision, or will you have responsibility for independent decisions in this work?

4) Choose appropriate study materials

Now that you know the subjects to be examined and the relative amount of each subject to be covered, you can choose suitable study materials. For beginning level jobs, or even advanced ones, if you have a pronounced weakness in some aspect of your training, read a modern, standard textbook in that field. Be sure it is up to date and has general coverage. Such books are normally available at your library, and the librarian will be glad to help you locate one. For entry-level positions, questions of appropriate difficulty are chosen – neither highly advanced questions, nor those too simple. Such questions require careful thought but not advanced training.

If the position for which you are applying is technical or advanced, you will read more advanced, specialized material. If you are already familiar with the basic principles of your field, elementary textbooks would waste your time. Concentrate on advanced textbooks and technical periodicals. Think through the concepts and review difficult problems in your field.

These are all general sources. You can get more ideas on your own initiative, following these leads. For example, training manuals and publications of the government agency which employs workers in your field can be useful, particularly for technical and professional positions. A letter or visit to the government department involved may result in more specific study suggestions, and certainly will provide you with a more definite idea of the exact nature of the position you are seeking.

III. KINDS OF TESTS

Tests are used for purposes other than measuring knowledge and ability to perform specified duties. For some positions, it is equally important to test ability to make adjustments to new situations or to profit from training. In others, basic mental abilities not dependent on information are essential. Questions which test these things may not appear as pertinent to the duties of the position as those which test for knowledge and information. Yet they are often highly important parts of a fair examination. For very general questions, it is almost impossible to help you direct your study efforts. What we can do is to point out some of the more common of these general abilities needed in public service positions and describe some typical questions.

1) General information

Broad, general information has been found useful for predicting job success in some kinds of work. This is tested in a variety of ways, from vocabulary lists to questions about current events. Basic background in some field of work, such as sociology or economics, may be sampled in a group of questions. Often these are principles which have become familiar to most persons through exposure rather than through formal training. It is difficult to advise you how to study for these questions; being alert to the world around you is our best suggestion.

2) Verbal ability

An example of an ability needed in many positions is verbal or language ability. Verbal ability is, in brief, the ability to use and understand words. Vocabulary and grammar tests are typical measures of this ability. Reading comprehension or paragraph interpretation questions are common in many kinds of civil service tests. You are given a paragraph of written material and asked to find its central meaning.

3) Numerical ability

Number skills can be tested by the familiar arithmetic problem, by checking paired lists of numbers to see which are alike and which are different, or by interpreting charts and graphs. In the latter test, a graph may be printed in the test booklet which you are asked to use as the basis for answering questions.

4) Observation

A popular test for law-enforcement positions is the observation test. A picture is shown to you for several minutes, then taken away. Questions about the picture test your ability to observe both details and larger elements.

5) Following directions

In many positions in the public service, the employee must be able to carry out written instructions dependably and accurately. You may be given a chart with several columns, each column listing a variety of information. The questions require you to carry out directions involving the information given in the chart.

6) Skills and aptitudes

Performance tests effectively measure some manual skills and aptitudes. When the skill is one in which you are trained, such as typing or shorthand, you can practice. These tests are often very much like those given in business school or high school courses. For many of the other skills and aptitudes, however, no short-time preparation can be made. Skills and abilities natural to you or that you have developed throughout your lifetime are being tested.

Many of the general questions just described provide all the data needed to answer the questions and ask you to use your reasoning ability to find the answers. Your best preparation for these tests, as well as for tests of facts and ideas, is to be at your physical and mental best. You, no doubt, have your own methods of getting into an exam-taking mood and keeping "in shape." The next section lists some ideas on this subject.

IV. KINDS OF QUESTIONS

Only rarely is the "essay" question, which you answer in narrative form, used in civil service tests. Civil service tests are usually of the short-answer type. Full instructions for answering these questions will be given to you at the examination. But in case this is your first experience with short-answer questions and separate answer sheets, here is what you need to know:

1) Multiple-choice Questions

Most popular of the short-answer questions is the "multiple choice" or "best answer" question. It can be used, for example, to test for factual knowledge, ability to solve problems or judgment in meeting situations found at work.

A multiple-choice question is normally one of three types—
- It can begin with an incomplete statement followed by several possible endings. You are to find the one ending which *best* completes the statement, although some of the others may not be entirely wrong.
- It can also be a complete statement in the form of a question which is answered by choosing one of the statements listed.

- It can be in the form of a problem – again you select the best answer.

Here is an example of a multiple-choice question with a discussion which should give you some clues as to the method for choosing the right answer:

When an employee has a complaint about his assignment, the action which will *best* help him overcome his difficulty is to
   A. discuss his difficulty with his coworkers
   B. take the problem to the head of the organization
   C. take the problem to the person who gave him the assignment
   D. say nothing to anyone about his complaint

In answering this question, you should study each of the choices to find which is best. Consider choice "A" – Certainly an employee may discuss his complaint with fellow employees, but no change or improvement can result, and the complaint remains unresolved. Choice "B" is a poor choice since the head of the organization probably does not know what assignment you have been given, and taking your problem to him is known as "going over the head" of the supervisor. The supervisor, or person who made the assignment, is the person who can clarify it or correct any injustice. Choice "C" is, therefore, correct. To say nothing, as in choice "D," is unwise. Supervisors have and interest in knowing the problems employees are facing, and the employee is seeking a solution to his problem.

2) True/False Questions

The "true/false" or "right/wrong" form of question is sometimes used. Here a complete statement is given. Your job is to decide whether the statement is right or wrong.

SAMPLE: A roaming cell-phone call to a nearby city costs less than a non-roaming call to a distant city.

This statement is wrong, or false, since roaming calls are more expensive.
This is not a complete list of all possible question forms, although most of the others are variations of these common types. You will always get complete directions for answering questions. Be sure you understand *how* to mark your answers – ask questions until you do.

V. RECORDING YOUR ANSWERS

Computer terminals are used more and more today for many different kinds of exams.
For an examination with very few applicants, you may be told to record your answers in the test booklet itself. Separate answer sheets are much more common. If this separate answer sheet is to be scored by machine – and this is often the case – it is highly important that you mark your answers correctly in order to get credit.
An electronic scoring machine is often used in civil service offices because of the speed with which papers can be scored. Machine-scored answer sheets must be marked with a pencil, which will be given to you. This pencil has a high graphite content which responds to the electronic scoring machine. As a matter of fact, stray dots may register as answers, so do not let your pencil rest on the answer sheet while you are pondering the correct answer. Also, if your pencil lead breaks or is otherwise defective, ask for another.

Since the answer sheet will be dropped in a slot in the scoring machine, be careful not to bend the corners or get the paper crumpled.

The answer sheet normally has five vertical columns of numbers, with 30 numbers to a column. These numbers correspond to the question numbers in your test booklet. After each number, going across the page are four or five pairs of dotted lines. These short dotted lines have small letters or numbers above them. The first two pairs may also have a "T" or "F" above the letters. This indicates that the first two pairs only are to be used if the questions are of the true-false type. If the questions are multiple choice, disregard the "T" and "F" and pay attention only to the small letters or numbers.

Answer your questions in the manner of the sample that follows:

32. The largest city in the United States is
    A. Washington, D.C.
    B. New York City
    C. Chicago
    D. Detroit
    E. San Francisco

1) Choose the answer you think is best. (New York City is the largest, so "B" is correct.)
2) Find the row of dotted lines numbered the same as the question you are answering. (Find row number 32)
3) Find the pair of dotted lines corresponding to the answer. (Find the pair of lines under the mark "B.")
4) Make a solid black mark between the dotted lines.

VI. BEFORE THE TEST

Common sense will help you find procedures to follow to get ready for an examination. Too many of us, however, overlook these sensible measures. Indeed, nervousness and fatigue have been found to be the most serious reasons why applicants fail to do their best on civil service tests. Here is a list of reminders:

- Begin your preparation early – Don't wait until the last minute to go scurrying around for books and materials or to find out what the position is all about.
- Prepare continuously – An hour a night for a week is better than an all-night cram session. This has been definitely established. What is more, a night a week for a month will return better dividends than crowding your study into a shorter period of time.
- Locate the place of the exam – You have been sent a notice telling you when and where to report for the examination. If the location is in a different town or otherwise unfamiliar to you, it would be well to inquire the best route and learn something about the building.
- Relax the night before the test – Allow your mind to rest. Do not study at all that night. Plan some mild recreation or diversion; then go to bed early and get a good night's sleep.
- Get up early enough to make a leisurely trip to the place for the test – This way unforeseen events, traffic snarls, unfamiliar buildings, etc. will not upset you.
- Dress comfortably – A written test is not a fashion show. You will be known by number and not by name, so wear something comfortable.

- Leave excess paraphernalia at home – Shopping bags and odd bundles will get in your way. You need bring only the items mentioned in the official notice you received; usually everything you need is provided. Do not bring reference books to the exam. They will only confuse those last minutes and be taken away from you when in the test room.
- Arrive somewhat ahead of time – If because of transportation schedules you must get there very early, bring a newspaper or magazine to take your mind off yourself while waiting.
- Locate the examination room – When you have found the proper room, you will be directed to the seat or part of the room where you will sit. Sometimes you are given a sheet of instructions to read while you are waiting. Do not fill out any forms until you are told to do so; just read them and be prepared.
- Relax and prepare to listen to the instructions
- If you have any physical problem that may keep you from doing your best, be sure to tell the test administrator. If you are sick or in poor health, you really cannot do your best on the exam. You can come back and take the test some other time.

VII. AT THE TEST

The day of the test is here and you have the test booklet in your hand. The temptation to get going is very strong. Caution! There is more to success than knowing the right answers. You must know how to identify your papers and understand variations in the type of short-answer question used in this particular examination. Follow these suggestions for maximum results from your efforts:

1) Cooperate with the monitor

The test administrator has a duty to create a situation in which you can be as much at ease as possible. He will give instructions, tell you when to begin, check to see that you are marking your answer sheet correctly, and so on. He is not there to guard you, although he will see that your competitors do not take unfair advantage. He wants to help you do your best.

2) Listen to all instructions

Don't jump the gun! Wait until you understand all directions. In most civil service tests you get more time than you need to answer the questions. So don't be in a hurry. Read each word of instructions until you clearly understand the meaning. Study the examples, listen to all announcements and follow directions. Ask questions if you do not understand what to do.

3) Identify your papers

Civil service exams are usually identified by number only. You will be assigned a number; you must not put your name on your test papers. Be sure to copy your number correctly. Since more than one exam may be given, copy your exact examination title.

4) Plan your time

Unless you are told that a test is a "speed" or "rate of work" test, speed itself is usually not important. Time enough to answer all the questions will be provided, but this does not mean that you have all day. An overall time limit has been set. Divide the total time (in minutes) by the number of questions to determine the approximate time you have for each question.

5) Do not linger over difficult questions

If you come across a difficult question, mark it with a paper clip (useful to have along) and come back to it when you have been through the booklet. One caution if you do this – be sure to skip a number on your answer sheet as well. Check often to be sure that you have not lost your place and that you are marking in the row numbered the same as the question you are answering.

6) Read the questions

Be sure you know what the question asks! Many capable people are unsuccessful because they failed to *read* the questions correctly.

7) Answer all questions

Unless you have been instructed that a penalty will be deducted for incorrect answers, it is better to guess than to omit a question.

8) Speed tests

It is often better NOT to guess on speed tests. It has been found that on timed tests people are tempted to spend the last few seconds before time is called in marking answers at random – without even reading them – in the hope of picking up a few extra points. To discourage this practice, the instructions may warn you that your score will be "corrected" for guessing. That is, a penalty will be applied. The incorrect answers will be deducted from the correct ones, or some other penalty formula will be used.

9) Review your answers

If you finish before time is called, go back to the questions you guessed or omitted to give them further thought. Review other answers if you have time.

10) Return your test materials

If you are ready to leave before others have finished or time is called, take ALL your materials to the monitor and leave quietly. Never take any test material with you. The monitor can discover whose papers are not complete, and taking a test booklet may be grounds for disqualification.

VIII. EXAMINATION TECHNIQUES

1) Read the general instructions carefully. These are usually printed on the first page of the exam booklet. As a rule, these instructions refer to the timing of the examination; the fact that you should not start work until the signal and must stop work at a signal, etc. If there are any *special* instructions, such as a choice of questions to be answered, make sure that you note this instruction carefully.

2) When you are ready to start work on the examination, that is as soon as the signal has been given, read the instructions to each question booklet, underline any key words or phrases, such as *least, best, outline, describe* and the like. In this way you will tend to answer as requested rather than discover on reviewing your paper that you *listed without describing*, that you selected the *worst* choice rather than the *best* choice, etc.

3) If the examination is of the objective or multiple-choice type – that is, each question will also give a series of possible answers: A, B, C or D, and you are called upon to select the best answer and write the letter next to that answer on your answer paper – it is advisable to start answering each question in turn. There may be anywhere from 50 to 100 such questions in the three or four hours allotted and you can see how much time would be taken if you read through all the questions before beginning to answer any. Furthermore, if you come across a question or group of questions which you know would be difficult to answer, it would undoubtedly affect your handling of all the other questions.

4) If the examination is of the essay type and contains but a few questions, it is a moot point as to whether you should read all the questions before starting to answer any one. Of course, if you are given a choice – say five out of seven and the like – then it is essential to read all the questions so you can eliminate the two that are most difficult. If, however, you are asked to answer all the questions, there may be danger in trying to answer the easiest one first because you may find that you will spend too much time on it. The best technique is to answer the first question, then proceed to the second, etc.

5) Time your answers. Before the exam begins, write down the time it started, then add the time allowed for the examination and write down the time it must be completed, then divide the time available somewhat as follows:
    - If 3-1/2 hours are allowed, that would be 210 minutes. If you have 80 objective-type questions, that would be an average of 2-1/2 minutes per question. Allow yourself no more than 2 minutes per question, or a total of 160 minutes, which will permit about 50 minutes to review.
    - If for the time allotment of 210 minutes there are 7 essay questions to answer, that would average about 30 minutes a question. Give yourself only 25 minutes per question so that you have about 35 minutes to review.

6) The most important instruction is to *read each question* and make sure you know what is wanted. The second most important instruction is to *time yourself properly* so that you answer every question. The third most important instruction is to *answer every question*. Guess if you have to but include something for each question. Remember that you will receive no credit for a blank and will probably receive some credit if you write something in answer to an essay question. If you guess a letter – say "B" for a multiple-choice question – you may have guessed right. If you leave a blank as an answer to a multiple-choice question, the examiners may respect your feelings but it will not add a point to your score. Some exams may penalize you for wrong answers, so in such cases *only*, you may not want to guess unless you have some basis for your answer.

7) Suggestions
    a. Objective-type questions
        1. Examine the question booklet for proper sequence of pages and questions
        2. Read all instructions carefully
        3. Skip any question which seems too difficult; return to it after all other questions have been answered
        4. Apportion your time properly; do not spend too much time on any single question or group of questions

5. Note and underline key words – *all, most, fewest, least, best, worst, same, opposite*, etc.
6. Pay particular attention to negatives
7. Note unusual option, e.g., unduly long, short, complex, different or similar in content to the body of the question
8. Observe the use of "hedging" words – *probably, may, most likely*, etc.
9. Make sure that your answer is put next to the same number as the question
10. Do not second-guess unless you have good reason to believe the second answer is definitely more correct
11. Cross out original answer if you decide another answer is more accurate; do not erase until you are ready to hand your paper in
12. Answer all questions; guess unless instructed otherwise
13. Leave time for review

b. Essay questions
1. Read each question carefully
2. Determine exactly what is wanted. Underline key words or phrases.
3. Decide on outline or paragraph answer
4. Include many different points and elements unless asked to develop any one or two points or elements
5. Show impartiality by giving pros and cons unless directed to select one side only
6. Make and write down any assumptions you find necessary to answer the questions
7. Watch your English, grammar, punctuation and choice of words
8. Time your answers; don't crowd material

8) Answering the essay question

Most essay questions can be answered by framing the specific response around several key words or ideas. Here are a few such key words or ideas:

M's: manpower, materials, methods, money, management
P's: purpose, program, policy, plan, procedure, practice, problems, pitfalls, personnel, public relations

a. Six basic steps in handling problems:
1. Preliminary plan and background development
2. Collect information, data and facts
3. Analyze and interpret information, data and facts
4. Analyze and develop solutions as well as make recommendations
5. Prepare report and sell recommendations
6. Install recommendations and follow up effectiveness

b. Pitfalls to avoid
1. *Taking things for granted* – A statement of the situation does not necessarily imply that each of the elements is necessarily true; for example, a complaint may be invalid and biased so that all that can be taken for granted is that a complaint has been registered

2. *Considering only one side of a situation* – Wherever possible, indicate several alternatives and then point out the reasons you selected the best one
3. *Failing to indicate follow up* – Whenever your answer indicates action on your part, make certain that you will take proper follow-up action to see how successful your recommendations, procedures or actions turn out to be
4. *Taking too long in answering any single question* – Remember to time your answers properly

IX. AFTER THE TEST

Scoring procedures differ in detail among civil service jurisdictions although the general principles are the same. Whether the papers are hand-scored or graded by machine we have described, they are nearly always graded by number. That is, the person who marks the paper knows only the number – never the name – of the applicant. Not until all the papers have been graded will they be matched with names. If other tests, such as training and experience or oral interview ratings have been given, scores will be combined. Different parts of the examination usually have different weights. For example, the written test might count 60 percent of the final grade, and a rating of training and experience 40 percent. In many jurisdictions, veterans will have a certain number of points added to their grades.

After the final grade has been determined, the names are placed in grade order and an eligible list is established. There are various methods for resolving ties between those who get the same final grade – probably the most common is to place first the name of the person whose application was received first. Job offers are made from the eligible list in the order the names appear on it. You will be notified of your grade and your rank as soon as all these computations have been made. This will be done as rapidly as possible.

People who are found to meet the requirements in the announcement are called "eligibles." Their names are put on a list of eligible candidates. An eligible's chances of getting a job depend on how high he stands on this list and how fast agencies are filling jobs from the list.

When a job is to be filled from a list of eligibles, the agency asks for the names of people on the list of eligibles for that job. When the civil service commission receives this request, it sends to the agency the names of the three people highest on this list. Or, if the job to be filled has specialized requirements, the office sends the agency the names of the top three persons who meet these requirements from the general list.

The appointing officer makes a choice from among the three people whose names were sent to him. If the selected person accepts the appointment, the names of the others are put back on the list to be considered for future openings.

That is the rule in hiring from all kinds of eligible lists, whether they are for typist, carpenter, chemist, or something else. For every vacancy, the appointing officer has his choice of any one of the top three eligibles on the list. This explains why the person whose name is on top of the list sometimes does not get an appointment when some of the persons lower on the list do. If the appointing officer chooses the second or third eligible, the No. 1 eligible does not get a job at once, but stays on the list until he is appointed or the list is terminated.

X. HOW TO PASS THE INTERVIEW TEST

The examination for which you applied requires an oral interview test. You have already taken the written test and you are now being called for the interview test – the final part of the formal examination.

You may think that it is not possible to prepare for an interview test and that there are no procedures to follow during an interview. Our purpose is to point out some things you can do in advance that will help you and some good rules to follow and pitfalls to avoid while you are being interviewed.

What is an interview supposed to test?

The written examination is designed to test the technical knowledge and competence of the candidate; the oral is designed to evaluate intangible qualities, not readily measured otherwise, and to establish a list showing the relative fitness of each candidate – as measured against his competitors – for the position sought. Scoring is not on the basis of "right" and "wrong," but on a sliding scale of values ranging from "not passable" to "outstanding." As a matter of fact, it is possible to achieve a relatively low score without a single "incorrect" answer because of evident weakness in the qualities being measured.

Occasionally, an examination may consist entirely of an oral test – either an individual or a group oral. In such cases, information is sought concerning the technical knowledges and abilities of the candidate, since there has been no written examination for this purpose. More commonly, however, an oral test is used to supplement a written examination.

Who conducts interviews?

The composition of oral boards varies among different jurisdictions. In nearly all, a representative of the personnel department serves as chairman. One of the members of the board may be a representative of the department in which the candidate would work. In some cases, "outside experts" are used, and, frequently, a businessman or some other representative of the general public is asked to serve. Labor and management or other special groups may be represented. The aim is to secure the services of experts in the appropriate field.

However the board is composed, it is a good idea (and not at all improper or unethical) to ascertain in advance of the interview who the members are and what groups they represent. When you are introduced to them, you will have some idea of their backgrounds and interests, and at least you will not stutter and stammer over their names.

What should be done before the interview?

While knowledge about the board members is useful and takes some of the surprise element out of the interview, there is other preparation which is more substantive. It *is* possible to prepare for an oral interview – in several ways:

1) Keep a copy of your application and review it carefully before the interview

This may be the only document before the oral board, and the starting point of the interview. Know what education and experience you have listed there, and the sequence and dates of all of it. Sometimes the board will ask you to review the highlights of your experience for them; you should not have to hem and haw doing it.

2) Study the class specification and the examination announcement

Usually, the oral board has one or both of these to guide them. The qualities, characteristics or knowledges required by the position sought are stated in these documents. They offer valuable clues as to the nature of the oral interview. For example, if the job involves supervisory responsibilities, the announcement will usually indicate that knowledge of modern supervisory methods and the qualifications of the candidate as a supervisor will be tested. If so, you can expect such questions, frequently in the form of a hypothetical situation which you are expected to solve. NEVER go into an oral without knowledge of the duties and responsibilities of the job you seek.

3) Think through each qualification required

Try to visualize the kind of questions you would ask if you were a board member. How well could you answer them? Try especially to appraise your own knowledge and background in each area, *measured against the job sought*, and identify any areas in which you are weak. Be critical and realistic – do not flatter yourself.

4) Do some general reading in areas in which you feel you may be weak

For example, if the job involves supervision and your past experience has NOT, some general reading in supervisory methods and practices, particularly in the field of human relations, might be useful. Do NOT study agency procedures or detailed manuals. The oral board will be testing your understanding and capacity, not your memory.

5) Get a good night's sleep and watch your general health and mental attitude

You will want a clear head at the interview. Take care of a cold or any other minor ailment, and of course, no hangovers.

What should be done on the day of the interview?

Now comes the day of the interview itself. Give yourself plenty of time to get there. Plan to arrive somewhat ahead of the scheduled time, particularly if your appointment is in the fore part of the day. If a previous candidate fails to appear, the board might be ready for you a bit early. By early afternoon an oral board is almost invariably behind schedule if there are many candidates, and you may have to wait. Take along a book or magazine to read, or your application to review, but leave any extraneous material in the waiting room when you go in for your interview. In any event, relax and compose yourself.

The matter of dress is important. The board is forming impressions about you – from your experience, your manners, your attitude, and your appearance. Give your personal appearance careful attention. Dress your best, but not your flashiest. Choose conservative, appropriate clothing, and be sure it is immaculate. This is a business interview, and your appearance should indicate that you regard it as such. Besides, being well groomed and properly dressed will help boost your confidence.

Sooner or later, someone will call your name and escort you into the interview room. *This is it.* From here on you are on your own. It is too late for any more preparation. But remember, you asked for this opportunity to prove your fitness, and you are here because your request was granted.

What happens when you go in?

The usual sequence of events will be as follows: The clerk (who is often the board stenographer) will introduce you to the chairman of the oral board, who will introduce you to the other members of the board. Acknowledge the introductions before you sit down. Do not be surprised if you find a microphone facing you or a stenotypist sitting by. Oral interviews are usually recorded in the event of an appeal or other review.

Usually the chairman of the board will open the interview by reviewing the highlights of your education and work experience from your application – primarily for the benefit of the other members of the board, as well as to get the material into the record. Do not interrupt or comment unless there is an error or significant misinterpretation; if that is the case, do not hesitate. But do not quibble about insignificant matters. Also, he will usually ask you some question about your education, experience or your present job – partly to get you to start talking and to establish the interviewing "rapport." He may start the actual questioning, or turn it over to one of the other members. Frequently, each member undertakes the questioning on a particular area, one in which he is perhaps most competent, so you can expect each member to participate in the examination. Because time is limited, you may also expect some rather abrupt switches in the direction the questioning takes, so do not be upset by it. Normally, a board member will not pursue a single line of questioning unless he discovers a particular strength or weakness.

After each member has participated, the chairman will usually ask whether any member has any further questions, then will ask you if you have anything you wish to add. Unless you are expecting this question, it may floor you. Worse, it may start you off on an extended, extemporaneous speech. The board is not usually seeking more information. The question is principally to offer you a last opportunity to present further qualifications or to indicate that you have nothing to add. So, if you feel that a significant qualification or characteristic has been overlooked, it is proper to point it out in a sentence or so. Do not compliment the board on the thoroughness of their examination – they have been sketchy, and you know it. If you wish, merely say, "No thank you, I have nothing further to add." This is a point where you can "talk yourself out" of a good impression or fail to present an important bit of information. Remember, *you close the interview yourself.*

The chairman will then say, "That is all, Mr. _____, thank you." Do not be startled; the interview is over, and quicker than you think. Thank him, gather your belongings and take your leave. Save your sigh of relief for the other side of the door.

How to put your best foot forward

Throughout this entire process, you may feel that the board individually and collectively is trying to pierce your defenses, seek out your hidden weaknesses and embarrass and confuse you. Actually, this is not true. They are obliged to make an appraisal of your qualifications for the job you are seeking, and they want to see you in your best light. Remember, they must interview all candidates and a non-cooperative candidate may become a failure in spite of their best efforts to bring out his qualifications. Here are 15 suggestions that will help you:

1) Be natural – Keep your attitude confident, not cocky

If you are not confident that you can do the job, do not expect the board to be. Do not apologize for your weaknesses, try to bring out your strong points. The board is interested in a positive, not negative, presentation. Cockiness will antagonize any board member and make him wonder if you are covering up a weakness by a false show of strength.

2) Get comfortable, but don't lounge or sprawl

Sit erectly but not stiffly. A careless posture may lead the board to conclude that you are careless in other things, or at least that you are not impressed by the importance of the occasion. Either conclusion is natural, even if incorrect. Do not fuss with your clothing, a pencil or an ashtray. Your hands may occasionally be useful to emphasize a point; do not let them become a point of distraction.

3) Do not wisecrack or make small talk

This is a serious situation, and your attitude should show that you consider it as such. Further, the time of the board is limited – they do not want to waste it, and neither should you.

4) Do not exaggerate your experience or abilities
In the first place, from information in the application or other interviews and sources, the board may know more about you than you think. Secondly, you probably will not get away with it. An experienced board is rather adept at spotting such a situation, so do not take the chance.

5) If you know a board member, do not make a point of it, yet do not hide it
Certainly you are not fooling him, and probably not the other members of the board. Do not try to take advantage of your acquaintanceship – it will probably do you little good.

6) Do not dominate the interview
Let the board do that. They will give you the clues – do not assume that you have to do all the talking. Realize that the board has a number of questions to ask you, and do not try to take up all the interview time by showing off your extensive knowledge of the answer to the first one.

7) Be attentive
You only have 20 minutes or so, and you should keep your attention at its sharpest throughout. When a member is addressing a problem or question to you, give him your undivided attention. Address your reply principally to him, but do not exclude the other board members.

8) Do not interrupt
A board member may be stating a problem for you to analyze. He will ask you a question when the time comes. Let him state the problem, and wait for the question.

9) Make sure you understand the question
Do not try to answer until you are sure what the question is. If it is not clear, restate it in your own words or ask the board member to clarify it for you. However, do not haggle about minor elements.

10) Reply promptly but not hastily
A common entry on oral board rating sheets is "candidate responded readily," or "candidate hesitated in replies." Respond as promptly and quickly as you can, but do not jump to a hasty, ill-considered answer.

11) Do not be peremptory in your answers
A brief answer is proper – but do not fire your answer back. That is a losing game from your point of view. The board member can probably ask questions much faster than you can answer them.

12) Do not try to create the answer you think the board member wants
He is interested in what kind of mind you have and how it works – not in playing games. Furthermore, he can usually spot this practice and will actually grade you down on it.

13) Do not switch sides in your reply merely to agree with a board member
Frequently, a member will take a contrary position merely to draw you out and to see if you are willing and able to defend your point of view. Do not start a debate, yet do not surrender a good position. If a position is worth taking, it is worth defending.

14) Do not be afraid to admit an error in judgment if you are shown to be wrong

The board knows that you are forced to reply without any opportunity for careful consideration. Your answer may be demonstrably wrong. If so, admit it and get on with the interview.

15) Do not dwell at length on your present job

The opening question may relate to your present assignment. Answer the question but do not go into an extended discussion. You are being examined for a *new* job, not your present one. As a matter of fact, try to phrase ALL your answers in terms of the job for which you are being examined.

Basis of Rating

Probably you will forget most of these "do's" and "don'ts" when you walk into the oral interview room. Even remembering them all will not ensure you a passing grade. Perhaps you did not have the qualifications in the first place. But remembering them will help you to put your best foot forward, without treading on the toes of the board members.

Rumor and popular opinion to the contrary notwithstanding, an oral board wants you to make the best appearance possible. They know you are under pressure – but they also want to see how you respond to it as a guide to what your reaction would be under the pressures of the job you seek. They will be influenced by the degree of poise you display, the personal traits you show and the manner in which you respond.

ABOUT THIS BOOK

This book contains tests divided into Examination Sections. Go through each test, answering every question in the margin. We have also attached a sample answer sheet at the back of the book that can be removed and used. At the end of each test look at the answer key and check your answers. On the ones you got wrong, look at the right answer choice and learn. Do not fill in the answers first. Do not memorize the questions and answers, but understand the answer and principles involved. On your test, the questions will likely be different from the samples. Questions are changed and new ones added. If you understand these past questions you should have success with any changes that arise. Tests may consist of several types of questions. We have additional books on each subject should more study be advisable or necessary for you. Finally, the more you study, the better prepared you will be. This book is intended to be the last thing you study before you walk into the examination room. Prior study of relevant texts is also recommended. NLC publishes some of these in our Fundamental Series. Knowledge and good sense are important factors in passing your exam. Good luck also helps. So now study this Passbook, absorb the material contained within and take that knowledge into the examination. Then do your best to pass that exam.

EXAMINATION SECTION

EXAMINATION SECTION
TEST 1

DIRECTIONS: Each question or incomplete statement is followed by several suggested answers or completions. Select the one that BEST answers the question or completes the statement. *PRINT THE LETTER OF THE CORRECT ANSWER IN THE SPACE AT THE RIGHT.*

1. A mass diagram is used in water supply computations to determine the
   A. size of the area that will be flooded when a dam is built
   B. capacity of reservoir required to supply the demand for water
   C. volume of excavation required to clear the site for a reservoir
   D. rate of flow of water into a reservoir

2. The velocity head in a pipe is equal to
   A. $\frac{v^2}{2g}$ B. $\frac{v^2}{g}$ C. $\frac{v}{2g}$ D. $\frac{v}{g}$

3. A force of 200 lbs. and a force of 300 lbs. make an angle of 30° with each other. The value of the resultant force is, in lbs., MOST NEARLY
   A. 483 B. 48 C. 493 D. 513

4. A chemical commonly used for coagulation in a water purification plant is
   A. alum B. caustic ash C. potash D. saltpeter

5. The consistency of a concrete mix is measured with a
   A. water meter   B. viscosimeter
   C. slump cone   D. vicat needle

6. The term *4000 pound concrete* commonly means
   A. one cubic yard of concrete weighs approximately 4000 pounds
   B. the allowable stress in compression in the concrete is 400 lb./sq.in.
   C. the concrete has a minimum ultimate strength in compression of 4000 lb./sq.in. at 28 days
   D. the concrete can carry a bond stress of 4000 lb./sq.in.

Questions 7-9.

DIRECTIONS: Questions 7 through 9 refer to the sketch of a reinforced concrete beam.

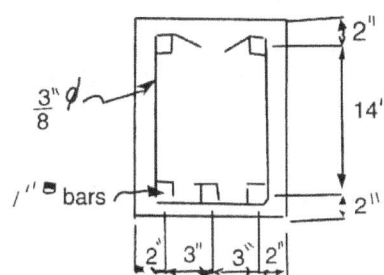

7. The effective width of the beam is, in inches, MOST NEARLY
   A. 5   B. 8   C. 9   D. 10

8. The ³/₈" diameter bar is _____ reinforcement.
   A. temperature   B. tension
   C. compression   D. shear

9. Provided no 1" bars are bent up, the upper two square bars are _____ reinforcement.
   A. temperature   B. tension
   C. compression   D. shear

10. The sine of 120° is the same as the sine of
    A. 45°   B. 60°
    C. 45°, but with a negative sign   D. 60° but with a negative sign

11. The formula for the area of a triangle is
    A. ½ab sin A   B. ½bc sin A   C. ½ac cos A   D. ½ab cos A

12. The logarithm of 7 is approximately 0.845.
    The logarithm of (0.007)¼ is APPROXIMATELY
    A. 9.343-10   B. 9.567-10   C. 9.461-10   D. 9.561-10

13. The center of gravity of a triangle is located at the intersection of the
    A. angle bisectors
    B. medians
    C. perpendicular bisectors of the sides
    D. radians

14. The distance between two stations was measured six times and the average distance found to be 346.215 ft.
    If one measurement of 351.205 ft. is deleted from the data as being inconsistent with the other measurements, then the average of the remaining five measurements is, in ft.,
    A. 345.217   B. 345.221   C. 345.227   D. 345.235

15. A ma of an area 380 ft. x 740 ft. is to be plotted on a sheet of drawing paper. The SMALLEST sheet of paper required to plot this map to a scale of 1" = 50', leaving a one inch margin all around, is, in inches,
    A. 8½ x 11   B. 10 x 17   C. 12 x 17   D. 10 x 15

16. On a topographic map, widely spaced contour lines indicate
    A. a gentle slope   B. a steep slope
    C. an overhanging cliff   D. the bank of a stream

17. The scale to which a map is drawn is 1" = 800'.
    Of the following, the MOST common method by which this scale would be
    indicated on the map is
    A. 1/800
    B. 1" = 9600"
    C. 8.0" = one mile
    D. 1/9600

18. The angle formed between one line and the prolongation of the preceding
    line in a closed traverse is known as a(n) _____ angle.
    A. split
    B. obtuse
    C. direction
    D. deflection

19. When laying out a horizontal circular curve, the deflection angle for a 100 ft.
    chord is equal to
    A. one-quarter of the degree of curvature
    B. one-half of the degree of curvature
    C. three-quarters of the degree of curvature
    D. the degree of curvature

20. For a given intersection angle, tables of the functions of a one degree curve
    show the tangent distance to be 1062.0 ft.
    For the same intersection angle and a curvature of 4°, the tangent distance is,
    in feet, MOST NEARLY
    A. 265.5
    B. 437.9
    C. 649.3
    D. 1153.4

21. The bending moment diagram for the beam
    shown in the diagram at the right is
    A. A
    B. B
    C. C
    D. D

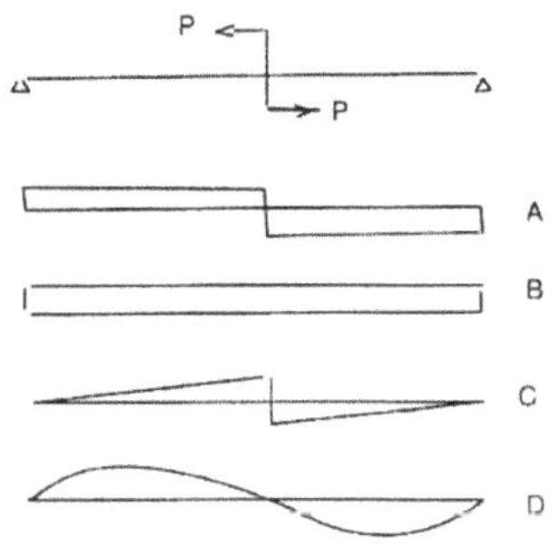

22. The bending moment at the center of a simple beam supporting a uniform load
    of w pounds per foot throughout its entire length, l, is
    A. $\frac{wl^2}{2}$
    B. $\frac{wl^2}{4}$
    C. $\frac{3wx^2}{8}$
    D. $\frac{wl^2}{8}$

23. A simple beam on a 16'0" span carries a concentrated load of 10,000 pounds.
    If the maximum bending moment in the beam is 465,000 inch pounds, the
    distance from the load to the nearer support is, in feet, MOST NEARLY
    A. 6.1
    B. 6.3
    C. 6.6
    D. 6.9

24. The section modulus of a rectangular beam 6 inches wide and 12 inches
    deep is, in inches cubed,
    A. 24
    B. 48
    C. 96
    D. 144

4 (#1)

25. A 6" x 8" timber (actual size) is to be used as a beam on a simple span. 25.____
If the 8-inch side is vertical rather than the 6-inch side, the beam is NOT
   A. stronger in bending   B. stronger in shear
   C. stiffer   D. more efficient

26. A 6" x 8" timber (actual size) is being used as a gin pole. 26.____
The radius of gyration of this column which would be used in a column formula
to determine safe load for the gin pole is, in inches, MOST NEARLY
   A. 1.73   B. 1.87   C. 1.93   D. 2.13

27. A steel rod 25'0" long and 1 inch square in cross-section, fastened to solid 27.____
supports, is under a tension of 18,000 lb./sq.in.
If one of the supports yields 0.14 inches, the resultant tension in the bar will be,
in pounds per square inch, MOST NEARLY ($E = 30 \times 10^6$ lb./sq.in.)
   A. 3800   B. 4000   C. 4200   D. 4400

28. A round steel bar, one inch in diameter and three feet long, is elongated 28.____
.022 inches by a load applied at one end of the bar.
The magnitude of the load is, in lbs., MOST NEARLY ($E = 30 \times 10^6$ lb./sq.in.)
   A. 14,200   B. 14,400   C. 14,600   D. 14,940

29. A short hollow steel cylinder with a wall thickness of 1.5 inches is to carry a 29.____
compressive load, applied uniformly on the end, of 1,750,000 lb.
If the allowable working stress in steel in comparison is 20,000 lb./sq.in., then
the minimum outside diameter of the cylinder required to safely support this
load is, in inches, MOST NEARLY
   A. 19.4   B. 19.8   C. 20.0   D. 20.2

Questions 30-31.

DIRECTIONS: Questions 30 and 31 are to be answered on the basis of the following frame.

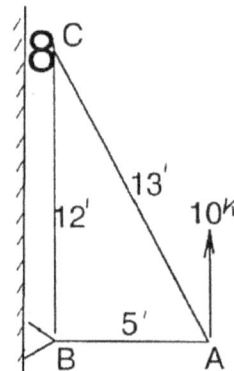

30. The reaction at joint C of the frame is, in kips, MOST NEARLY 30.____
   A. 4.17   B. 4.29   C. 4.37   D. 4.63

31. The stress in member BC of the frame is, in kips, MOST NEARLY 31.____
   A. 10.0   B. 10.6   C. 10.8   D. 11.2

32. The modulus of elasticity of aluminum is one-third that of steel. 32.____
This means that
   A. steel is three times as strong as aluminum
   B. aluminum is lighter than steel
   C. aluminum is three times as strong as steel
   D. for equal stress intensities, the unit strain in aluminum is three times that in steel

Questions 33-35.

DIRECTIONS: Questions 33 through 35 are to be answered on the basis of the following stress-strain diagram.

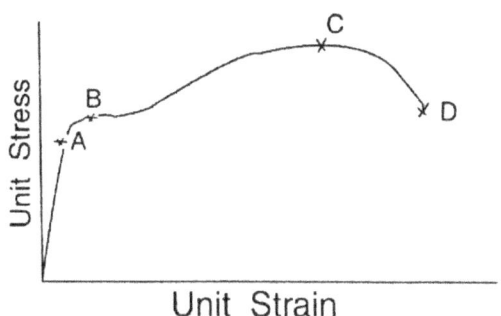

33. The stress-strain diagram is for 33.____
   A. high-carbon steel   B. low-carbon steel
   C. cast iron   D. concrete

34. The yield point is marked 34.____
   A. A   B. B   C. C   D. D

35. The ultimate strength is marked 35.____
   A. A   B. B   C. C   D. D

Questions 36-37.

DIRECTIONS: Questions 36 and 37 are to be answered on the basis of the following sketch.

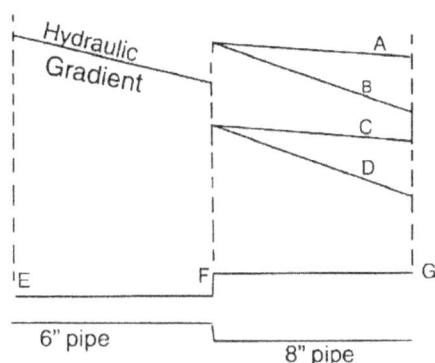

36. The velocity of flow in section EF is 6'/sec.
    The velocity of flow in section FG is, in feet per second, MOST NEARLY
    A. 3.36   B. 3.38   C. 3.40   D. 3.44

37. If the hydraulic gradient as shown from E to F, the hydraulic gradient from F to G is marked
    A. A   B. B   C. C   D. D

38. A 6-inch pipe line is horizontal from point A to point B, the distance AB being 2000 feet. At A, the hydraulic gradient is 10 feet above the pipe; at B it is 2 feet below the pipe.
    The head lost per thousand feet is, in feet,
    A. 1   B. 3   C. 7   D. 6

39. A canal is to have a cross-sectional area of 60 square feet.
    If a square cross-section is used, the hydraulic radius of the canal when flowing full will be, in feet, MOST NEARLY
    A. 2.41   B. 2.45   C. 2.51   D. 2.58

40. If one cubic foot of cement weighs 94 pounds and the specific gravity of the cement particles is 3.10, the void ratio (ratio of volume of voids to volume of solids) is MOST NEARLY
    A. 0.89   B. 0.96   C. 1.03   D. 1.06

KEY (CORRECT ANSWERS)

1.	B	11.	B	21.	C	31.	A
2.	A	12.	C	22.	D	32.	D
3.	A	13.	B	23.	C	33.	B
4.	A	14.	A	24.	D	34.	B
5.	C	15.	B	25.	B	35.	C
6.	C	16.	A	26.	A	36.	B
7.	D	17.	D	27.	B	37.	A
8.	D	18.	D	28.	B	38.	D
9.	C	19.	B	29.	C	39.	D
10.	B	20.	A	30.	A	40.	D

SOLUTIONS TO PROBLEMS

3. CORRECT ANSWER: A

   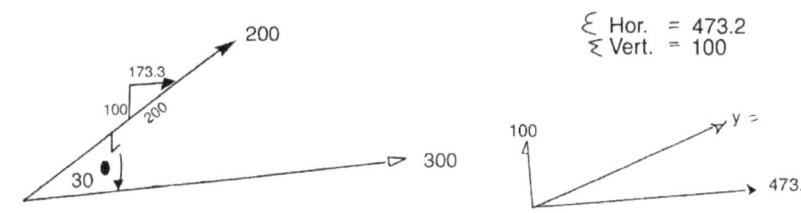

   r = $\sqrt{100^2 + 473.2^2}$ = 483 lbs.

10. CORRECT ANSWER: B

    sin A = sin(π-A); sin 120° = sin 60°

11. CORRECT ANSWER: B

    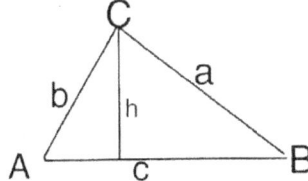

    sin A = h/b
    Area = $(\frac{1}{2})(c)(h) = \frac{1}{2}$bc sin A

12. CORRECT ANSWER: C

    Log $(0.007)\frac{1}{4} = \frac{1}{4}$log 7 × 10⁻³ = $\frac{1}{4}$(-3+0.845) = 0.539 or 9.461-10

14. CORRECT ANSWER: A

    [(6)(346.215) − 351.205]/5 = 1826.085/5 = 365.217

15. CORRECT ANSWER: A
    Each dimension on paper must be increased by two inches (one inch margin on each side); 380/50 ~ 8, 740/50 ~ 15 or 10 × 17

19. CORRECT ANSWER: B
    Deflection angles for 100 ft. lengths are multiples of ½ degree of curvature.

20. CORRECT ANSWER: A
    Since degree of curve is described by the angle subtended by a chord or are of 100 ft. length, the tangent distance is a direct measure of the degree of curve. For 4°, (1062.0)(¼) = 265.5 ft.

8 (#1)

22. CORRECT ANSWER: D

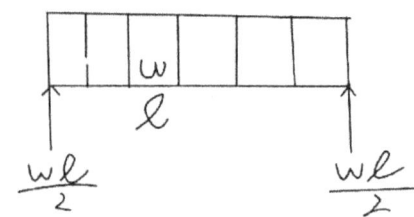

Moment @ $\frac{1}{2}$ = $\frac{wl}{2}\frac{(1)}{(2)}$ - $\frac{wl}{2}\frac{(1)}{(4)}$

from the rt.

$= \frac{wl^2}{4} - \frac{wl^2}{8}$

$= \frac{wl^2}{8}$

23. CORRECT ANSWER: C

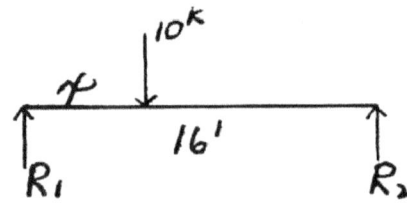

$M = \frac{465000}{12} = 38.750$ ft.-k

$R_1 = \frac{(16-x)}{(16)} 10$

$38.75 = R_1 x = \frac{(16-x)}{(16)}(10)(x) = \frac{160x - 10x^2}{16}$

$10x^2 - 160x + 38.75(16) = 0$

$x^2 - 16x + 62 = 0$

$x = \frac{-b \pm \sqrt{b^2 - 4ac}}{2a}$

$x = \frac{16 \pm \sqrt{256 - 248}}{2} = \frac{16 \pm \sqrt{8}}{2}$

$x = 8 \pm \sqrt{2}$

It must be less than 8 to be the distance to the nearer support ∴ 8 − 1.4 = 6.6

24. CORRECT ANSWER: D

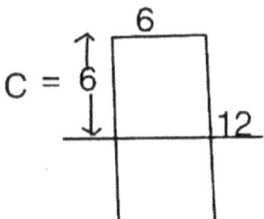

Section Modulus $= \frac{1}{c}$

$I = \frac{bh^3}{12} = \frac{6 \times 12^3}{12} = 6 \times 12^2$

$c = 6$

$\frac{1}{c} = \frac{6 \times 12^2}{6}$ $12^2 = 144$

25. CORRECT ANSWER: B
By having the 8-inch side vertical rather than the 6-inch side, it becomes stronger in bending, stiffer and more efficient, but the shear strength remains the same.

26. CORRECT ANSWER: A

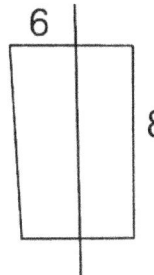

(taken about the weak axis)

$r = \dfrac{d}{\sqrt{12}}$

$d = 6$

$r = \dfrac{6}{\sqrt{12}}$ 1.73

27. CORRECT ANSWER: B
$E = 30 \times 10^6$
$A = \pi/4$
$\varepsilon = \dfrac{\sigma}{E} = \dfrac{18000}{30 \times 10^6} = 600 \times 10^{-6}$

Support yield = 0.14 inches = $\dfrac{0.14}{25 \times 12} = 467 \times 10^{-6}$

$(600-467) \times 10^{-6} = 133$ in/in

$\sigma = E\varepsilon = 30 \times 10^6 \times 133 \times 10^{-6} = 3990$ psi

28. CORRECT ANSWER: B
$E = 30 \times 10^6$ psi

$A = \dfrac{\pi D^2}{4} = \pi/4$ in^2

$\varepsilon = .022/36 = 611 \times 10^{-6}$ in/in

$\sigma = \dfrac{P}{A} = P/\pi/4$

$E = \dfrac{\sigma}{\varepsilon}$

$p = E\varepsilon \pi/4 = 30 \times 10^6 \times 611 \times 10^6 \times \pi/4 = 14{,}400$ lbs.

29. CORRECT ANSWER: C

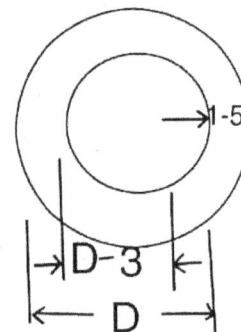

$A = \dfrac{P}{\sigma} = \dfrac{1,750,000 \text{ lbs.}}{20,000 \text{ psi}} = 87.5 \text{ in}^2$

$\dfrac{\pi D^2}{4} - \dfrac{\pi(D-3)^2}{4} = 87.5$

$D^2 - (D^2 - 6D + 9) = 8.75(4/\pi)$

$6D = 111.4 + 9$
$D = 20.07$

30. CORRECT ANSWER: A
Horizontal reaction C from ΣM about B =
C(12) = 10 × 5
C→ = 4.17

31. CORRECT ANSWER: A
$\Sigma V = 0$; BC takes only the vertical loading because of the roller at B.

32. CORRECT ANSWER: D
$E = \dfrac{\sigma}{\varepsilon}$

Steel E ≈ 30
AlE ≈ 10

$\varepsilon \text{steel} = \dfrac{\sigma \text{const}}{30} = 1/30$

$\varepsilon \text{al} = \dfrac{\sigma \text{const}}{10} = 1/10$

$\dfrac{1 \text{ al}}{10} = 3(\dfrac{1 \text{st}}{30})$

33. CORRECT ANSWER: B
Low carbon steel because of the ductility

36. CORRECT ANSWER: B
Q = flow (ft 3/sec.)   Q = Av
A = area(ft^2)   Av = A'v
v = velocity (ft/sec) $(9\pi)(6) = (16\pi)v$
                            v = 3.38

37. CORRECT ANSWER: A
The hydraulic gradient is a line drawn through a series of points to which water would rise in piezometer tubes attached to a pipe through which water flows. The head loss in the larger pipe due to friction will be at a lesser rate than the smaller pipe because of the larger diameter and lower velocity of flow.

39. CORRECT ANSWER: D

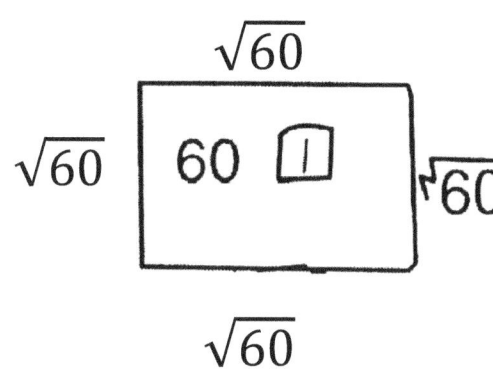

hydraulic radius = $\dfrac{\text{cross-section area of water}}{\text{wetted perimeter}}$

$= \dfrac{60}{3\sqrt{60}} = 2.58$

40. CORRECT ANSWER: D
    If there were no voids, the weight of one cubic ft. would be 3.10 × 62.4 = 193.44

Volume of voids = $\dfrac{193.44-94}{193.44}$ ft³ = $\dfrac{99.44}{193.44}$

Volume of solids = $\dfrac{94}{193.44}$ ft³

Void ratio = $\dfrac{99.44}{94.00}$ = 1.06

TEST 2

DIRECTIONS: Each question or incomplete statement is followed by several suggested answers or completions. Select the one that BEST answers the question or completes the statement. *PRINT THE LETTER OF THE CORRECT ANSWER IN THE SPACE AT THE RIGHT.*

1. A *plane table* is MOST commonly used to
   A. determine trigonometric functions of angles
   B. plot large maps in the office from data taken in the field
   C. plot maps directly in the field
   D. adjust distances from slope measurements to horizontal measurements

   1.____

2. Of the following formulas used in taping, the one that gives the correction for sag is
   A. $\dfrac{h^2}{2s}$
   B. $\dfrac{0.204W\sqrt{AE}}{\sqrt{P_n - P_o}}$
   C. $\dfrac{(P-P_o)l}{AE}$
   D. $\dfrac{W^2L}{24P^2}$

   2.____

3. Recorded distances will be less than the actual horizontal distances when measurements are taken
   A. with the tape on a slope
   B. at a temperature lower than that at which the tape was standardized
   C. with the center of the tape out of line
   D. with a tension greater than that at which the tape was standardized

   3.____

4. A 100 ft. steel tape is standardized fully supported under a 10 pound pull when the temperature is 59°F and found to be 100.17 feet long. A distance of 70.00 feet is to be laid out with this tape under the standardization conditions.
   The tape distance to lay out, in feet, is
   A. 69.88   B. 69.99   C. 70.01   D. 70.12

   4.____

5. In the closed traverse ABC, the bearings of lines AB and BC are N45°-00'E and N60°00'E, respectively. The lengths of these lines are 200 ft. and 300 ft., respectively. The bearing of line CA is MOST NEARLY
   A. S54°-00'W   B. S56°-00'W   C. S58°-00'W   D. S60°-00'W

   5.____

6. A transit is so designed that the stadia constant C is negligible. The stadia interval factor is 200. When the telescope if level,
   A. readings must be taken on the stadia red every 100 ft.
   B. the distance from the instrument to the rod is 100 times the difference between the readings of the upper and lower crosshairs on the rod
   C. the scale used to read the stadia rod is divided into 100 parts
   D. the difference of elevation from the instrument to the point on which the rod is held is equal to the stadia reading plus 1.00 ft.

   6.____

Questions 7-11.

DIRECTIONS: In Questions 7 through 11, the plan and front elevation of an object are shown on the left, and on the right are shown four figures, one of which, and only one, represents the right side elevation. Indicate the letter which represents the right side elevation.

SAMPLE QUESTION: In the sample shown below, which figure correctly represents the right side elevation?

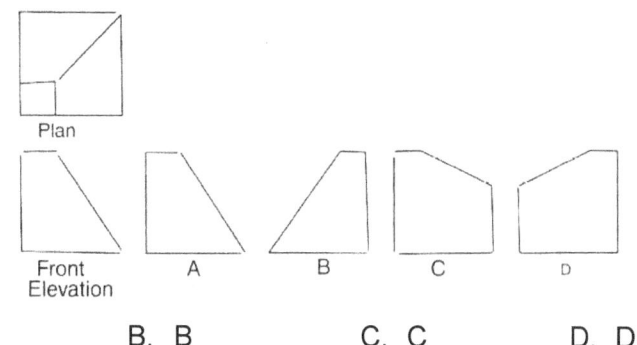

A. A
B. B
C. C
D. D

The correct answer is A.

7.

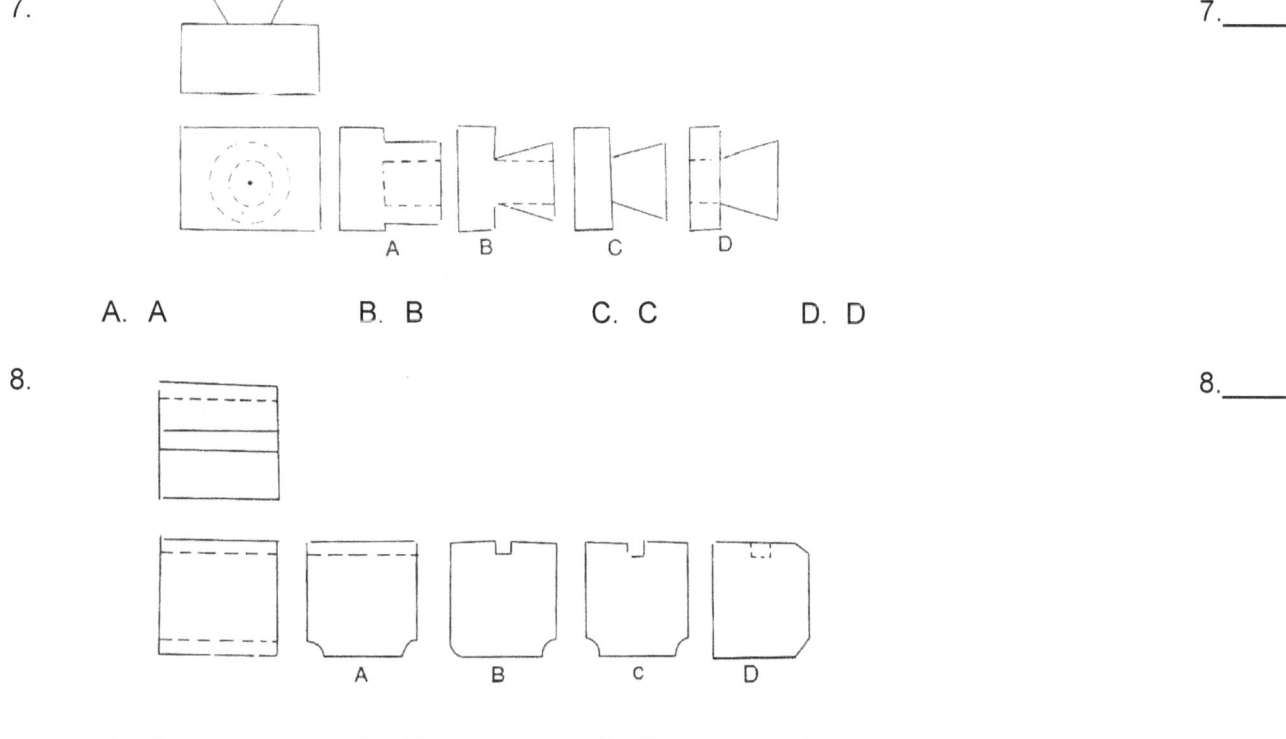

A. A
B. B
C. C
D. D

8.

A. A
B. B
C. C
D. D

9. 9.____

A. A B. B C. C D. D

10. 10.____

A. A B. B C. C D. D

11. 11,____

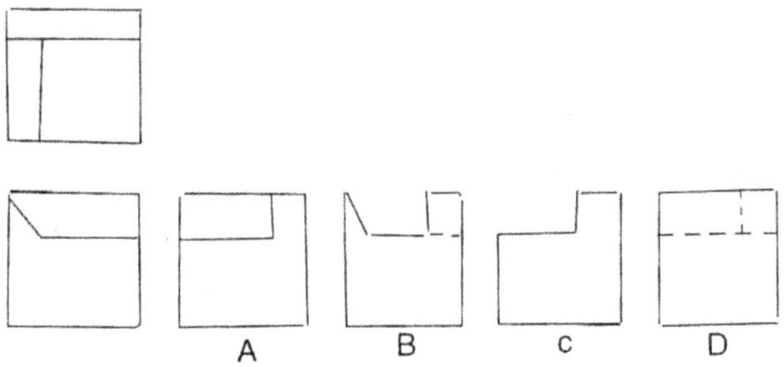

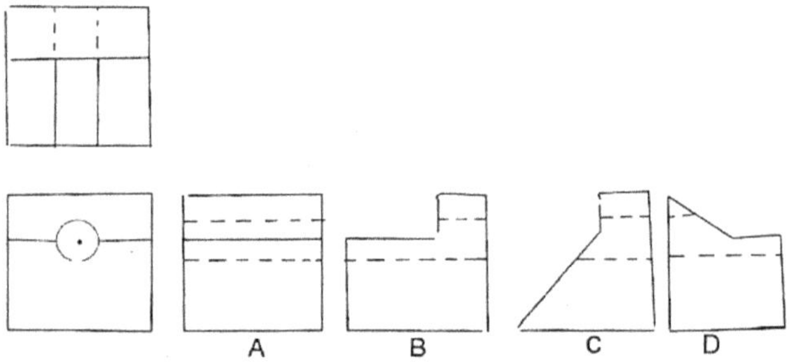

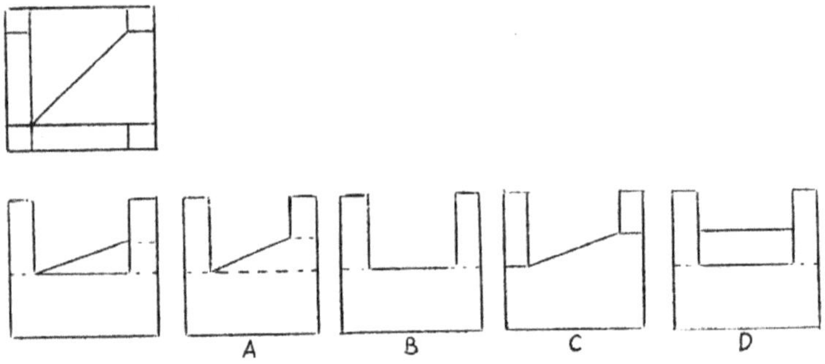

A. A B. B C. C D. D

Questions 12-14.

DIRECTIONS: Questions 12 through 14 are to be answered on the basis of the following sketch.

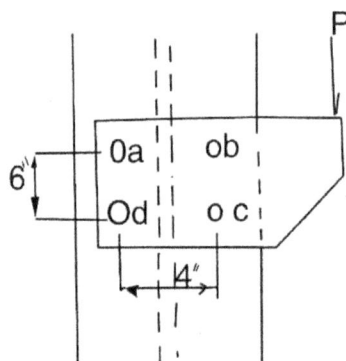

4 (#2)

12. Maximum rivet stress occurs in rivet 12.____
    A. a only   B. b only   C. c only   D. b and c

13. The plate carrying the load is known as a _____ plate. 13.____
    A. gusset   B. flange   C. web   D. shear

14. The plate carrying the load is attached to a(n) _____ column. 14.____
    A. built-up   B. H
    C. channel   D. none of the above

15. A 3 x 3 x ³/₈ angle in a structural frame is in tension. It is connected at each 15.____
    end by one ⁷/₈" rivet to a gusset plate.
    The net section of the angle is equal to the gross minus _____ square inches.
    A. 0.339   B. 0.347   C. 0.375   D. 0.389

16. A formula commonly used to determine the allowable unit stresses in columns 16.____
    is s =

    A. $\frac{\pi^2 EI}{4I^2}$

    B. $17000 - .485(\frac{1}{r})^2$

    C. $\frac{22500}{1+\frac{l^2}{1800r^2}}$

    D. $\frac{P+Mc}{A \pm I}$

17. A rectangular footing 6'0" long by 4'0" wide carries a vertical load of 20,000 17.____
    pounds located on the long axis 5 inches from the center of the footing.
    The maximum soil pressure under the footing due to this load is, in pounds per
    square inch, MOST NEARLY
    A. 1250   B. 1350   C. 1450   D. 1550

18. *Special anchorage* in concrete work commonly refers to 18.____
    A. reinforcement in concrete bolted to steel girders
    B. wing walls on a retaining wall to provide extra support
    C. a hook at the end of a reinforcing rod in continuous beam construction
    D. additional steel dowels connecting a concrete column with a concrete
       footing

Questions 19-20.

DIRECTIONS: Questions 19 and 20 are to be answered on the basis of the following sketch.

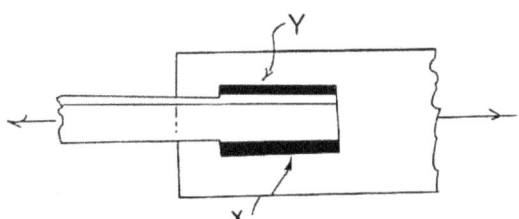

19. In the welded section shown, the length of weld x should be _____ that of y. 19.____
    A. equal to   B. greater than
    C. less than   D. independent of

20. The welds shown are _____ welds. 20.____
    A. single V   B. double V   C. plug   D. fillet

21. The slope at any point on the bending moment diagram for a beam is equal 21.____
    to the _____ the beam at that point.
    A. load on   B. shear on
    C. deflection of   D. slope of

22. The shear diagram for the beam shown in the diagram at the right is 22.____
    A. A
    B. B
    C. C
    D. D

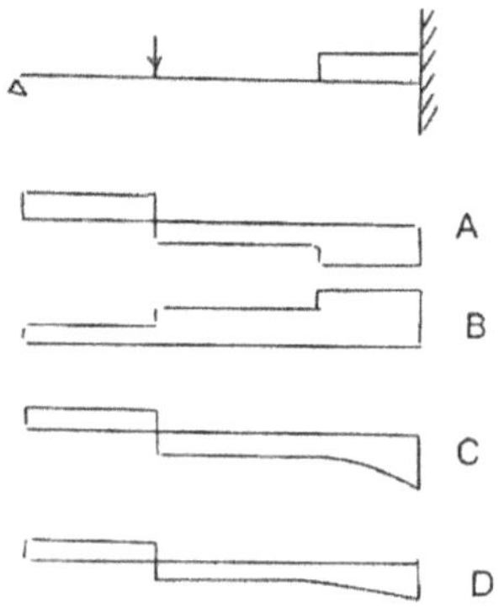

23. Vertical curves in highway work are usually parts of 23.____
    A. circles   B. ellipses   C. hyperbolas   D. parabolas

24. In laying out an angle with a transit, an error of one minute will result in 24.____
    locating a point 1000 ft. from the transit off the true line by APPROXIMATELY _____ ft.
    A. 0.1   B. 0.2   C. 0.3   D. 0.5

25. The sum of the positive departures of a closed traverse exceeds that of the 25.____
    negative departures by 0.31 ft. The sum of the negative latitudes exceeds that
    of the positive latitudes by 0.67 ft.
    The linear error of closure is, in feet, MOST NEARLY
    A. 0.39   B. 0.47   C. 0.58   D. 0.74

26. The balanced latitudes and departures of the sides of a closed traverse are 26.____
    as follows:

Line	Lat.	Dep.
AB	+152.27	+212.06
BC	+316.19	+ 83.92
CD	-522.34	+119.30
DA	+ 53.88	-415.28

    The DMD of line CD referred to a meridian through A is
    A. 567.89   B. 635.46   C. 711.26   D. 819.77

Questions 27-31.

DIRECTIONS: Questions 27 through 31 are to be answered on the basis of the following closed traverse which is drawn to scale.

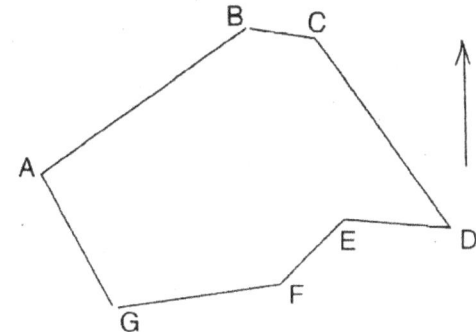

27. The sum of the interior angles of the traverse is
    A. 760° B. 844° C. 900° D. 920°

    27.____

28. The arithmetical sum of the deflection angles, i.e., the sum without regard to sign, is
    A. 160°
    B. 240°
    C. 330°
    D. greater than 360°

    28.____

29. When balancing a survey of a closed traverse, the functions of angles most commonly used are
    A. sin and tan   B. cos and tan   C. sin and cos   D. tan and cot

    29.____

30. Of the following lines, the one with the LARGEST departure is
    A. AB B. CD C. AG D. GF

    30.____

31. The area of the traverse could not be computed if all sides and angles were measured EXCEPT
    A. angles A, B, and C
    B. sides AB and CD and angle B
    C. side AB and angles A and B
    D. sides AB, BC, and CD

    31.____

32. The notes for a level run are as follows:

Sta.	BS	HI	FS	Elev.
BM1	3.26			100.23
A	2.13		1.19	
B	4.05		3.20	
C	2.26		4.03	
BM2			4.22	

    The elevation of BMS is
    A. 99.17 B. 99.21 C. 99.25 D. 99.29

    32.____

33. The foot of a leveling rod has been worn through hard use so that the rod is now .02 ft. short.
    The elevation of any point found, using this rod, will be
    A. .02 ft. low   B. correct   C. .02 ft. high   D. .04 ft. high

34. The correction to be applied to high rod readings on a Philadelphia rod is -0.004. In running a level circuit with this rod,
    A. 0.004 should be subtracted from all high rod readings before entering them
    B. the error should be ignored as it will cancel itself
    C. the error should be ignored until all elevations are computed and then corrections should be made to elevations as required
    D. the total error will be 0.004 times the square root of the number of high rod readings

Questions 35-40.

DIRECTIONS: Questions 35 through 40 are to be answered on the basis of the following sketch of a transit.

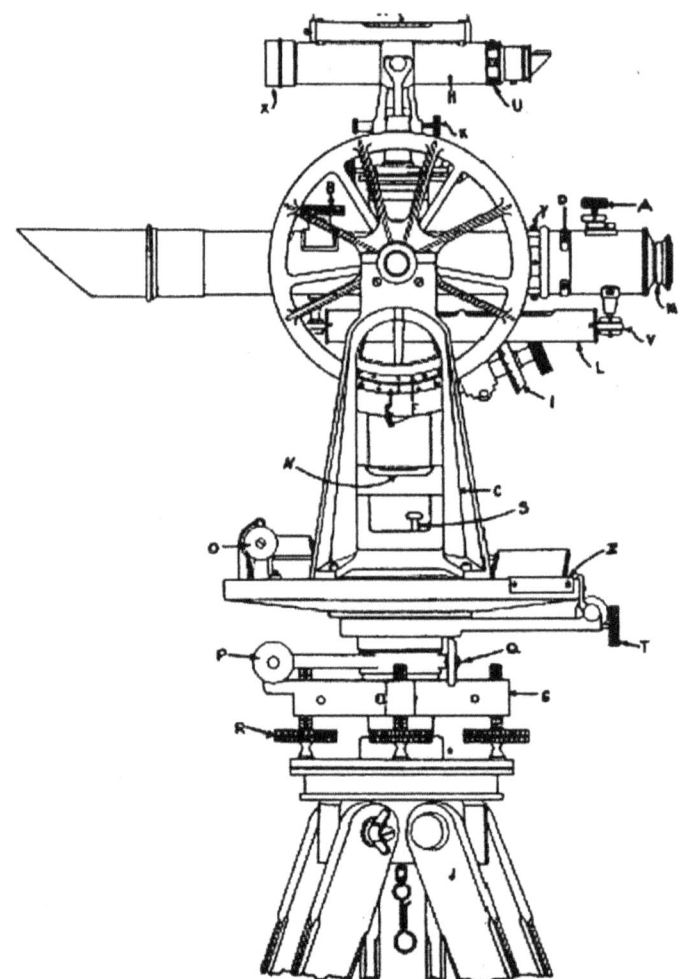

35. The vertical circle is marked
   A. D B. E C. F D. I

36. A prism would be attached at
   A. M B. U C. X D. Z

37. The lower motion clamp is marked
   A. K B. P C. Q D. T

38. The bubble which would normally be centered to make the line of sight truly horizontal is marked
   A. L B. N C. O D. W

39. The needle lifting or needle release screw is marked
   A. D B. K C. R D. S

40. A peg test for this transit has been performed, and the line of sight reads 4.085 on the far rod. The far rod reading is computed to be 4.060. In making the adjustment, the first thing to move is the
   A. bubble adjusting screws
   B. capstan-headed screws on the reticule
   C. vertical slow motion
   D. vertical Vernier adjusting screws

KEY (CORRECT ANSWERS)

1.	C	11.	A	21.	B	31.	D
2.	D	12.	D	22.	D	32.	D
3.	D	13.	A	23.	D	33.	B
4.	A	14.	B	24.	C	34.	C
5.	A	15.	C	25.	D	35.	C
6.	B	16.	B	26.	C	36.	A
7.	C	17.	A	27.	C	37.	C
8.	B	18.	C	28.	D	38.	A
9.	A	19.	C	29.	C	39.	D
10.	B	20.	D	30.	A	40.	C

SOLUTIONS TO PROBLEMS

3. **CORRECT ANSWER: D**
   The tapes' lengths are based on a standardized tension. If extra tension is applied, a short reading will result.

4. **CORRECT ANSWER: A**
   The correction to be applied is:
   70/100 × .17 = 0.12
   ∴ 70.00 − 0.12 = 69.88

5. **CORRECT ANSWER: A**
   200 ft. @ N45°E = 2 × 45 = 90°
   300 ft. @ N60°E = $\frac{3}{5}$ × 60 = $\frac{180°}{270°}$

   AC = $\frac{270°}{5}$ = N54°E
   CA = S54°W

6. **CORRECT ANSWER: B**
   This is the definition of the stadia interval factor.

12. **CORRECT ANSWER: D**
    The rivet stress is derived from the vertical load and the moment derived thereof. In this case, the vertical load is equal and the stresses due to moment are equal and additive to the vertical load. The moment stress is subtractive from the stresses on a and d.

15. **CORRECT ANSWER: C**
    The net section = the gross minus the area taken by the rivet 1/8" larger than the rivet used.

    The area subtracted = (8/8+1/8) × 3/8 = 0.375 in².

    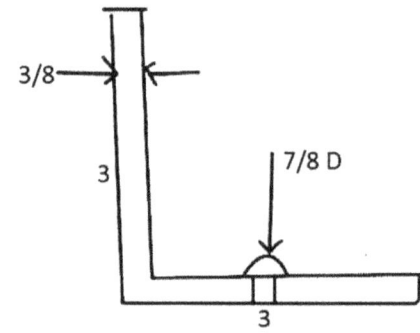

17. **CORRECT ANSWER: A**
    Max. stress = P/A + $\frac{MC}{I}$ C = 3
    I = bh³/12

    = $\frac{20}{6 \times 4} + \frac{(20 \times \frac{1}{2})(3)}{\frac{4 \times 6^3}{12}}$

    = $\frac{20}{24} + \frac{15}{36}$ = .83 + .42 = 1.25K psf = 1250 psf

    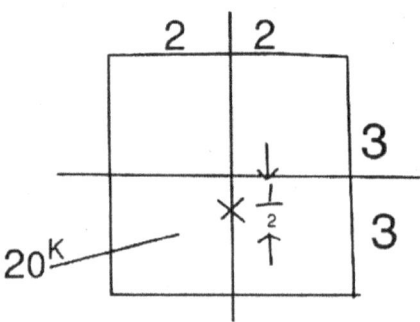

23. CORRECT ANSWER: D
Parabolic arc is ideally suited for changes in vertical grade since slope varies at constant rate with respect to horizontal distance.

24. CORRECT ANSWER: C
tan 1 minute = 0.00029

α = 1 minute
b = 1000 ft.
$\frac{a}{b}$ = tanα

a = tanα × b = .00029 × 1000 ft. = 0.29 ft.

25. CORRECT ANSWER: D

Linear error of closure $= \sqrt{(\Sigma \text{Lat})^2 + (\Sigma \text{Dep})^2}$

$= \sqrt{(0.31)^2 + (.67)^2}$

$= \sqrt{5450}$

= 0.74 ft.

26. CORRECT ANSWER: C
AB DMD = 212.06
BC DMD = 212.06 + 212.06 + 83.92 = 508.04
CD DMD = 508.04 + 83.92 + 119.30 = 711.26

The DMD of the first line equals the departure of the first line. The DMD of any other line is equal to the DMD of the preceding line plus the departure of the preceding line, plus the departure of the line itself.

27. CORRECT ANSWER: C
(n-2) × 180° = sum of the interior angles
n = number of sides
(7-2) × 180 = 900°

31. CORRECT ANSWER: D
There is no way to determine the lengths of these sides. All other missing data could be computed by trigonometry and geometry.

11 (#2)

32. CORRECT ANSWER: D
The complete notes should read as follows:

Sta.	BS	HI	FS	Elev.
BM1	3.26	103.49		100.23
A	2.13	104.43	1.19	102.30
B	4.05	105.28	3.20	101.23
C	2.26	103.51	4.03	101.25
BM2			4.22	99.29

33. CORRECT ANSWER: B
Elevations are determined by differences of rod readings; therefore, a short rod does not affect the final data.

TEST 3

DIRECTIONS: Each question or incomplete statement is followed by several suggested answers or completions. Select the one that BEST answers the question or completes the statement. *PRINT THE LETTER OF THE CORRECT ANSWER IN THE SPACE AT THE RIGHT.*

1. A wooden beam is a rectangle 6" x 12".
   On a simple span, the ratio of the uniform load it can carry with the 6" sides vertical to that with the 12" sides vertical is as one is to
   A. 2   B. 5   C. 7   D. 9

2. A moving load consists of a 4-kip and an 8-kip concentrated load spaced 8 feet apart.
   The maximum bending moment caused by this moving load on a simple span of 16 feet is, in kip-feet,
   A. 33.3   B. 31.9   C. 27.6   D. 23.9

3. A canal with a trapezoidal cross-section is 6'0" wide at the bottom and has side slopes of one on one.
   When the depth of water is 4'6", the hydraulic radius is
   A. 2.43   B. 2.52   C. 2.55   D. 2.67

4. The minimum amount of cover required for water mains in city streets is NOT affected by
   A. depth of frost
   B. consideration of shock loads
   C. depth of rock
   D. any of the above

5. A vertical steel tank, 10'0" diameter, wall thickness ¼", is subjected to a hydrostatic pressure of 100 feet of water. The maximum tensile stress in the tank, in lb./sq.in., is MOST NEARLY
   A. 10,200   B. 10,400   C. 10,600   D. 10,800

6. Three eye bars, 6" x 1" x 25'0", jointly, are to carry a load of 200,000 lbs. The middle bar is .03 inch too short. Assuming the pins through the eyes to be parallel, the cross-section of the bars to be uniform throughout their entire length, and $E = 30 \times 10^6$ #/sq.in., the stress in the outer bars in lb./sq.in. will be MOST NEARLY
   A. 10,100   B. 10,300   C. 10,500   D. 10,800

7. A property of steel NOT usually determined in the ordinary commercial tensile test of steel is
   A. modulus of rupture
   B. percent reduction in area
   C. yield point
   D. ultimate stress

8. In the activated sludge process, *seeding* is carried on in the
   A. grit chamber
   B. aeration tank
   C. sand filter
   D. sedimentation tank

9. The hydraulic radius is defined as
   A. the distance from the center of gravity of cross-sectional area of flow to the point of minimum velocity
   B. the cross-sectional area of waterway divided by the wetted perimeter
   C. half the depth of flow
   D. the depth from the free surface to the point of maximum velocity

10. Water flowing from an orifice in the side of a tank strikes the ground at a point 10 feet, below the orifice and 5 feet from the tank.
    If the coefficient of velocity is 1.00, the height of water above the orifice, in feet, is MOST NEARLY
    A. .63   B. 1.73   C. 3.5   D. 7.9

11. Of the following formulas, the one that is MOST commonly used in determining the runoff from a watershed is Q =
    A. $A \frac{1.486}{M} R^{2/3} S^{1/2}$ B. Aci C. $CLH^{3/2}$ D. $AC\sqrt{RS}$

12. Maximum discharge in a circular sewer occurs when the ratio of the depth of flow to the diameter of the pipe is MOST NEARLY
    A. .5   B. .6   C. .9   D. 1.1

13. Of the following items, the one that is LEAST important in the design of a concrete pier is
    A. corrosion   B. erosion   C. scour   D. elutriation

14. Of the following items, the one which is LEAST related to the others is
    A. extensometer   B. weir
    C. piezometer   D. hook gauge

15. In a through truss bridge, a horizontal longitudinal member acting as a beam to support loads is known as a
    A. floor beam   B. portal brace
    C. lower chord   D. stringer

16. Using pipe A alone, a given tank is filled with water in 5 minutes. When pipe B is used alone, the same tank is filled in 7 minutes.
    If both pipes are used at the same time, the length of time required to fill this tank is, in minutes, MOST NEARLY
    A. 2.87   B. 2.92   C. 2.99   D. 3.05

17. In plane surveying, double meridian distances are used to compute the _____ of a traverse.
    A. latitudes and departures
    B. area
    C. error of closure
    D. corrections for magnetic declination for the sides

18. The deflection angle required to lay out a 50 ft. chord of a 3°00' circular curve is MOST NEARLY
    A. 0°45' B. 1°45' C. 2°30' D. 3°45'

19. Of the following, the one that is NOT a method of locating details for topography is
    A. offset distance
    B. range line
    C. tie line
    D. string line

20. *Blocking in* is a practice followed when it is necessary to
    A. set up a transit on line between two stations
    B. prolong a line around an obstacle
    C. project a high point to the ground
    D. set a point on line by double centering

21. Of the following terms, the one that is LEAST related to the others is
    A. five level section
    B. slope stake
    C. mass diagram
    D. hydraulic fill

22. Using a given 100 foot tape, the slope distance between two points on a 2% grade is found to be 250.26. When checked later, the tape is found to be 100.02 ft. long.
    The horizontal distance between the two points is MOST NEARLY
    A. 250.21 B. 250.26 C. 250.29 D. 250.32

23. When it is impossible to balance the foresight and backsight distances, precise difference in elevations may be obtained by _____ leveling.
    A. trigonometric
    B. reciprocal
    C. stadia
    D. barometric

24. Specifications usually require that controlled concrete develop its design strength
    A. when forms are stripped
    B. in 28 days
    C. in 7 days
    D. in 2 months

25. Horizontal reinforcing in the exposed face of a cantilever retaining wall is necessary PRIMARILY to reinforce against _____ stress.
    A. tensile
    B. compressive
    C. shearing
    D. shrinkage

KEY (CORRECT ANSWERS)

1. A
2. A
3. B
4. C
5. B

6. A
7. A
8. B
9. B
10. A

11. B
12. C
13. D
14. A
15. D

16. B
17. B
18. A
19. D
20. A

21. D
22. B
23. B
24. C
25. D

EXAMINATION SECTION
TEST 1

DIRECTIONS: Each question or incomplete statement is followed by several suggested answers or completions. Select the one that BEST answers the question or completes the statement. *PRINT THE LETTER OF THE CORRECT ANSWER IN THE SPACE AT THE RIGHT.*

1. Dowels connecting adjacent roadway slabs are used primarily to

    A. transmit compressive stress to adjacent slabs
    B. reinforce against temperature stress
    C. reinforce against shrinkage stress
    D. prevent differential settlement of slabs

2. Good practice requires that the minimum overhead clearance at the crown for an underpass at the intersection of two highways be MOST NEARLY _____ feet.

    A. 10   B. 14   C. 17   D. 19

3. A simple beam on an 18'0" span carries a uniformly distributed load including its own weight of 200 pounds per foot.
   If a jack is placed under the midspan and the midpoint jacked up so it is at the same elevation as the ends, the load on the jack, in pounds, will be

    A. 960
    C. 1800
    B. 1600
    D. more than 1800

4. Of the following, the one which is NOT the symbol for a standard beam connection is

    A. A3   B. B3   C. H3   D. T3

5. Of the following items, the one that is NOT important in determining the minimum length of vertical curve required to connect two intersecting grades is

    A. maximum speed of vehicle
    B. grades of tangents
    C. whether intersection is at a summit or a sag
    D. crown of road

6. For an angle of intersection of 16°30', tables of the functions of a one-degree curve show the middle ordinate to be 59.30 feet.
   For the same angle of intersection, the middle ordinate for a curve whose radius is 1433 feet is MOST NEARLY

    A. 14.83   B. 24.94   C. 67.35   D. 183.72

7. The *Proctor Test* is used in testing

    A. asphalt   B. concrete   C. soils   D. mortar

8. Within the cross-section of a WF beam, the horizontal shearing stress is a maximum at the

A. midpoint of the beam
B. outermost fiber of the compression flange
C. outermost fiber of the tension flange
D. point of intersection of web and flange

9. The maximum load allowed on a 3/8" fillet weld, 6" long, when the allowable shearing stress is 13,000 #/sq.in. is MOST NEARLY, in pounds,

   A. 20,700   B. 21,900   C. 24,300   D. 26,370

10. A closed level circuit was run starting at BM A. The elevation of A on closing the circuit was found to be 0.097 lower than at the start.
    Of the following, the MOST logical reason for this error, barring mistakes, is the

    A. length of the rod was not standard due either to a uniform expansion or contraction
    B. level settled after the backsights had been read
    C. turning points settled after the foresights had been read
    D. line of sight was inclined upward and each foresight distance exceeded the corresponding backsight distance

11. The sensitivity of the bubble tube of an engineer's level can best be measured by

    A. measuring the distance between etched lines on the vial
    B. taking readings on a rod a known distance away with bubble in two different positions
    C. making a two-peg test
    D. measuring the curvature of the etched surface of the vial

12. Of the following, the MOST important source of accidental error in ordinary leveling work is

    A. change in length of leveling rod due to change in temperature
    B. axis of level tube not perpendicular to vertical axis
    C. eye piece is not focused accurately
    D. failure to wave rod

13. When taking a single measure of the horizontal angle between two points which differ greatly in elevation, the MOST important of the following relationships in the transit is

    A. axis of long bubble parallel to line of sight
    B. transverse axis perpendicular to vertical axis
    C. index correction of vertical arc equal to zero
    D. vertical cross-hair in plane perpendicular to transverse axis

14. Of the following factors, the one that is LEAST important in determining the total amount of superelevation required at the edge of pavement on a horizontal curve is

    A. speed of vehicle   B. weight of vehicle
    C. radius of curve   D. width of pavement

15. If the horizontal circle of a transit is graduated to 20' and 39 divisions on the limb equal 40 civisions on the vernier, then the LEAST count of the vernier is

    A. 14"   B. 28"   C. 30"   D. 1'6"

3 (#1)

16. The slump test for concrete is used to determine the

    A. strength B. consistency
    C. water ratio D. segregation

17. The following notes are taken from the survey of a closed traverse with five sides:

    △ at   Deflection Angles
    A   R 65° 25'
    B   L 45° 14'
    C   R 135° 42'
    D   R 92° 17'
    E

    The value of the deflection angle at E is MOST NEARLY

    A. 111°22' B. 111°34' C. 111°46' D. 111°50'

18. A Williot-Mohr diagram is used to determine

    A. deflection in trusses
    B. wind stress in framed bents
    C. diagonal shear in beams
    D. uplift pressure on the base of a cam

19. A reinforced concrete beam is 10" wide by 16" effective depth. If f_s = 20,000 lb./sq.in., f_c = 1350 lb./sq.in. and n = 10, then the value of k is MOST NEARLY

    A. .367 B. .373 C. .403 D. .419

20. Of the following concrete structures, the one in which gunite is MOST likely to be used is

    A. footings B. piles C. walls D. beams

21. For soil sampling in hardpan, the BEST method to use is

    A. jet probing B. wash boring
    C. auger boring D. core boring

22. The bending moment at the ends of a beam fully restrained at both ends which supports a uniform load of w pounds per foot throughout its entire length l is

    A. $\dfrac{wl^2}{8}$ B. $\dfrac{wl}{10}$ C. $\dfrac{wl^2}{10}$ D. $\dfrac{wl^2}{12}$

23. A reinforced concrete beam 10" wide by 16" effective depth is subjected to an end shear of 15,000 lbs.
    If f_s = 20,000 #/sq.in., f_c = 2500 #/sq.in., u = 187 #/sq.in., and j = .857, the perimeter of steel required to reinforce against the shear, in inches, is MOST NEARLY

    A. 2.38 B. 3.72 C. 5.85 D. 6.94

24. A precast reinforced concrete beam 20'0" long, weight 50 #/ft. is to be lifted by two slings symmetrically placed.
    For minimum bending stress in the beam, the distance from an end to a point of support, in feet, is MOST NEARLY

A. 3.98   B. 4.15   C. 4.35   D. 5.15

25. For maximum stress in *ab*, the distance the load *P* should be from the wall is MOST NEARLY
    A. 10'7"
    B. 11'9"
    C. 13'3"
    D. 15'0"

25._____

KEY (CORRECT ANSWERS)

1. D
2. B
3. D
4. D
5. D

6. A
7. C
8. A
9. A
10. D

11. B
12. C
13. B
14. B
15. C

16. B
17. D
18. A
19. C
20. C

21. D
22. D
23. C
24. B
25. D

TEST 2

DIRECTIONS: Each question or incomplete statement is followed by several suggested answers or completions. Select the one that BEST answers the question or completes the statement. *PRINT THE LETTER OF THE CORRECT ANSWER IN THE SPACE AT THE RIGHT.*

1. The rod reading at Sta. 100+27 is 4.26. With the same H.I., the rod reading at Sta. 103+16 is 6.34.
   The grade between the two stations is MOST NEARLY

   A. +0.72% B. +0.79% C. -0.72% D. -0.79%

   1.____

2. In taping a distance known to be 2000 ft. long, the distance is found to be 1900.02 ft.
   The error is MOST probably caused by

   A. neglecting temperature correction
   B. neglecting to record one tape length
   C. tension on tape not standard
   D. wind blowing tape out of line

   2.____

3. The sum of the deflection angles for a closed traverse, where *n* equals the number of sides of the traverse, is

   A. (n-2)180° B. 180°n C. (n-1)360° D. 360°

   3.____

4. When a level rod is *waved,* the correct reading is the

   A. largest reading
   B. smallest reading
   C. average of the largest and the smallest reading
   D. difference between the largest and the smallest reading

   4.____

5. A topographic map to a scale of 1:2400 has a 5-foot vertical interval. A straight line on the map connecting two adjacent contours is 0.437 inches long.
   The slope of this line is, in percent, MOST NEARLY

   A. 5.6 B. 5.7 C. 5.8 D. 6.0

   5.____

6. A Philadelphia rod is fully extended and the distance from the 1-foot mark to the 11-foot mark is measured and found to be 10.005.
   In a level circuit, a high-rod reading on this rod is

   A. 0.005 too large
   B. 0.005 too small
   C. considered correct since the errors will balance out
   D. correct if the rod is waved

   6.____

7. A differential leveling circuit without sideshots was run between two bench marks. The level was set up x times.
   The number of turning points used was

   A. 2x B. x-2 C. x-1 D. x

   7.____

8. A closed traverse is usually preferred to an open traverse because

   8.____

A. more ground can be covered
B. a mathematical check on the work is provided
C. the area can be determined
D. the computations are easier

9. The difference in elevation between two points on the hydraulic gradient of a pipe of uniform diameter is a measure of the loss of _____ head.

    A. potential   B. pressure   C. velocity   D. total

10. Of the following values of f in the formula $h = f \dfrac{l}{d} \dfrac{V^2}{2g}$, the one which would MOST probably apply to a smooth pipe is

    A. 0.02   B. 0.11   C. 0.31   D. 0.41

11. The required cross-sectional area of a culvert is a function of

    A. width of roadway   B. depth of fill
    C. drainage area served   D. headwall area

12. The value of k for a particular reinforced concrete beam is 0.400. The value of j for this beam is MOST NEARLY

    A. 0.873   B. 0.870   C. 0.867   D. 0.865

13. A steel bar one inch in diameter is imbedded a distance of 30 inches in a mass of concrete.
    If the bar is subjected to axial pull of 10,000#, the bond stress is, in pounds per square inch, MOST NEARLY

    A. 106   B. 108   C. 112   D. 116

14. The slump test for concrete is a measure of

    A. water-cement ratio   B. consistency
    C. strength   D. size of aggregate

15. The term *special anchorage* in concrete construction refers to

    A. an anchor bolt to tie a beam to a wall
    B. tieing the reinforcement to a steel beam
    C. a *U*-shaped bar to take care of shearing stresses
    D. a hook at the end of a reinforcing bar

16.

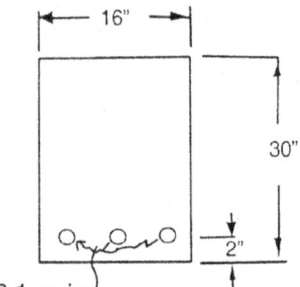

6.1 sq.in total

$k = \dfrac{1}{2} f_c k2j = 236$

Assuming exactly balanced design, the maximum bending moment that can be carried by the reinforced concrete beam in the accompanying sketch is, in inch pounds, MOST NEARLY

A. 2,960,000   B. 3,420,370   C. 4,160,500   D. 5,180,600

17. The maximum deflection of a simple beam on a span l carrying a uniformly distributed load of w per unit length is $\dfrac{5}{384}\dfrac{w}{EI}$ multiplied by

    A. l^2 B. l^3 C. l^4 D. l^7

18. The section modulus of a beam is

    A. $\int y^2 dA$ B. $\dfrac{V}{Ib}A\bar{y}$ C. $\dfrac{\sqrt{I}}{A}$ D. $\dfrac{I}{c}$

19. A timber beam 3" x 12" (actual dimensions) is simply supported on a clear span of 9'0" and carries a uniform load of 1000 #/ft. throughout its entire length.
    The maximum bending stress in the beam is, in lbs./sq.in., MOST NEARLY

    A. 1570   B. 1690   C. 1745   D. 1860

20. A wooden beam 8 inches wide by 12 inches deep (actual dimensions) carries a uniform load of 600 pounds per foot including its own weight on a simple span of 16'0".
    The MAXIMUM shear stress intensity in the beam is, in pounds per square inch,

    A. 70   B. 71   C. 72   D. 75

21. The horizontal component of the reaction at joint B in the accompanying diagram is MOST NEARLY

    A. $_{32}K$
    B. $_{36}K$
    C. $_{40}K$
    D. $_{44}K$

    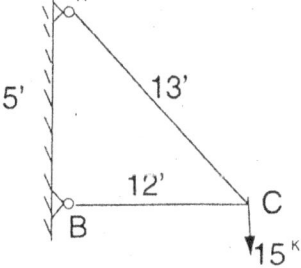

22. The yield point of a ductile metal is that unit stress at which

    A. the stress ceases to be proportional to the strain
    B. there is an increase in deformation with no increase in stress
    C. the material ruptures
    D. the metal ceases to act as an elastic material

Questions 23-27.

DIRECTIONS: Questions 23 through 27 refer to the sketch of the beam and girder connection shown below.

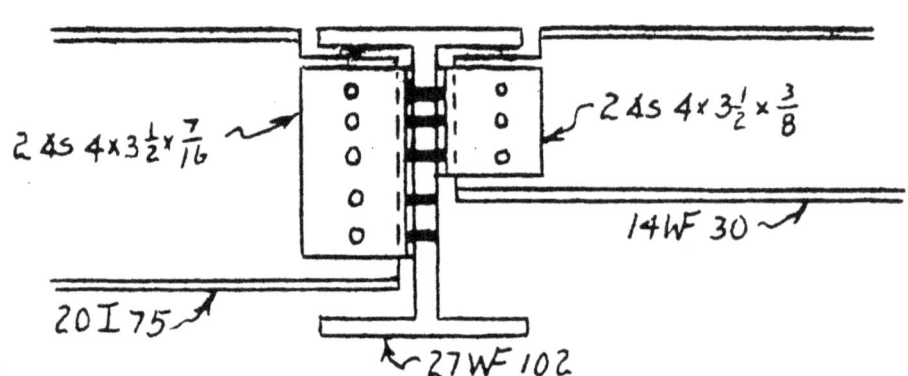

23. The diameter of the rivets used would MOST likely be

    A. 5/8"   B. 7/8"   C. 1 3/16"   D. 1 5/8"

24. Of the following allowable stresses, the only one that would be used in determining the number of rivets connecting the angles to the 20 I 75 is the allowable stress in

    A. single shear B. end bearing
    C. web shear D. enclosed bearing

25. The allowable load on rivet A is determined by the allowable stress in

    A. double shear B. single shear
    C. tension D. torsion

26. Both beams shown are

    A. chased   B. blocked   C. squared   D. clipped

27. The number of field rivets required in the connection is

    A. 4   B. 6   C. 9   D. 10

28. The term *batter* in concrete work refers to

    A. bracing of forms
    B. slope of finished surface
    C. consistency of concrete
    D. pressure of wet concrete in forms

29. Of the following items, the one that is LEAST related to the others is

    A. B.O.D. B. Imhoff tank
    C. effluent D. liquid limit

30. A beam on a simple span of 16'0" carries a concentrated load of 20 kips 5'0" from the left support and a uniform load of 3 kips per foot over the entire span.
    The distance from the left support to the point of maximum moment is, in feet, MOST NEARLY

    A. 5.92   B. 5.97   C. 6.02   D. 6.07

31. A beam has a trapezoidal cross-section which is symmetrical about a vertical axis. The top width is 4 inches, the bottom width 8 inches, and the depth 6 inches.
    The distance from the bottom of the beam to the neutral axis is, in inches,

A. 2.83   B. 2.75   C. 2.67   D. 2.59

32. The ends of a steel bar 1 inch square are set in rigid walls spaced 4'0" in the clear. Another square steel bar 2 inches on a side is set in rigid walls spaced 8'0" in the clear. The ratio of the unit stress in the longer bar to that in the shorter bar due to an increase in temperature is

    A. 3/8   B. 5/8   C. 1   D. 3/2

Questions 33-35.

DIRECTIONS: Questions 33 through 35 refer to the truss shown below.

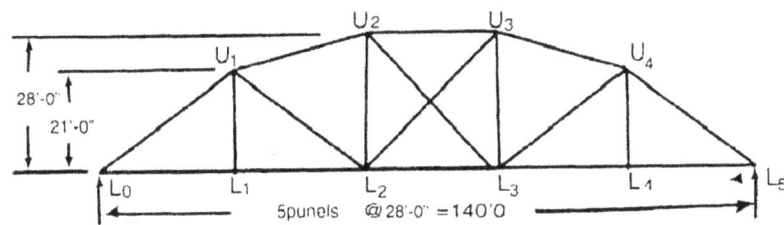

33. To obtain the stress in U_1L_2, the truss should be cut between U_1L_1 and U_2L_2 and moments taken about

    A. U_2
    B. L_1
    C. L_0
    D. a point to the left of L_0

34. The stress in member L_1L_2 for a load of one kip per foot extending over the entire span is, in kips, MOST NEARLY

    A. 74.67   B. 75.33   C. 75.67   D. 76.00

35. The stress in member U_2U_3 for a load of one kip per foot extending over the entire span is, in kips, MOST NEARLY

    A. 83.15   B. 83.30   C. 83.45   D. 84.00

36. In taping a distance on a 6% slope, the slope distance was measured. The correction per hundred feet to be applied to the measured distance is, in feet,

    A. 0.09   B. 0.12   C. 0.15   D. 0.18

37. The linear error of closure of a traverse is computed to be 0.04 feet. The sura of the lengths of the sides is 793.26 ft.
    The precision of the survey should be recorded as

    A. $\dfrac{0.04}{600}$ B. $\dfrac{4}{79326}$ C. $\dfrac{4}{793.26}$ D. $\dfrac{1}{19800}$

38. Errors due to eccentricity in the plates of a transit can be eliminated by

   A. reading the angle twice, once with the telescope normal, the second time with the telescope inverted
   B. using the averaged reading of the A and B verniers
   C. accurate leveling of the transit
   D. using two observers

39. A transit is set up at Sta. B and the deflection angle to Sta. C is measured (backsight on Sta. A) and found to be 22°15' R.
   The value of the angle ABC, measured clockwise from A to C, is

   A. 69°30'   B. 108°45'   C. 144°15'   D. 202°15'

40. The elevations of the P.V.C., P.V.I., and P.V.T. of a symnetrical vertical curve are 100.26, 103.26, and 98.76, respectively.
   The elevation of the midpoint of the vertical curve is MOST NEARLY

   A. 98.63   B. 99.72   C. 101.38   D. 103.17

KEY (CORRECT ANSWERS)

1. C	11. C	21. B	31. C
2. B	12. C	22. B	32. C
3. D	13. A	23. B	33. D
4. B	14. B	24. D	34. A
5. B	15. D	25. B	35. D
6. A	16. A	26. B	36. D
7. C	17. C	27. D	37. D
8. B	18. D	28. B	38. B
9. D	19. B	29. D	39. D
10. A	20. D	30. A	40. C

TEST 3

DIRECTIONS: Each question or incomplete statement is followed by several suggested answers or completions. Select the one that BEST answers the question or completes the statement. *PRINT THE LETTER OF THE CORRECT ANSWER IN THE SPACE AT THE RIGHT.*

1. In highway work, the degree of curve is commonly defined as the angle 1.____

    A. at the center subtended by an arc 100 ft. in length
    B. at the center subtending the entire curve
    C. at which the two tangents to the curve intersect
    D. between a tangent and a chord 100 ft. in length

2. The term *magnetic declination* refers to the 2.____

    A. attraction on a magnetic needle of nearby metallic objects
    B. dip of a magnetic needle
    C. angle between a given line and the meridian
    D. angle between true north and magnetic north

3. The bearings of the sides of a closed quadrilateral are: 3.____
    AB - N12°15'W
    BC - N15°10'E
    CD - S60°20'E
    DA - S18°30'W
    The interior angle CDA of the quadrilateral is

    A. 87°25'   B. 10°110'   C. 126°40'   D. 154°15'

4. In a given triangle, side *a* = 220 ft. and the angle opposite is 30°00'. 4.____
    If angle *B* = 45°00', then the side opposite angle *B*, in feet, is MOST NEARLY

    A. 311   B. 327   C. 346   D. 411

5. Of the following statements, the one that is CORRECT is: 5.____

    A. Blue ink is used when making tracings for blueprint work
    B. If ink lines on a tracing do not dry quickly, they should be blotted
    C. Vertical dimensions should be lettered so that they read from the right side of the sheet
    D. Dimension lines should be of the same weight as lines used in the views

6. A common method of lengthening the life of a wooden pile is by impregnating it with 6.____

    A. white lead   B. red lead
    C. sodium silicate   D. creosote

7. The MOST common unit for measuring excavation is 7.____

    A. cubic yard   B. cubic foot
    C. ton   D. pound

2 (#3)

8. The width of each lane in a modern two-lane highway would MOST likely be   8._____

   A. 8'   B. 12'   C. 16'   D. 20'

Questions 9-11.

DIRECTIONS: Questions 9 through 11 refer to the figure shown below. (Any trigonomatic computation required is to be done by slide rule.)

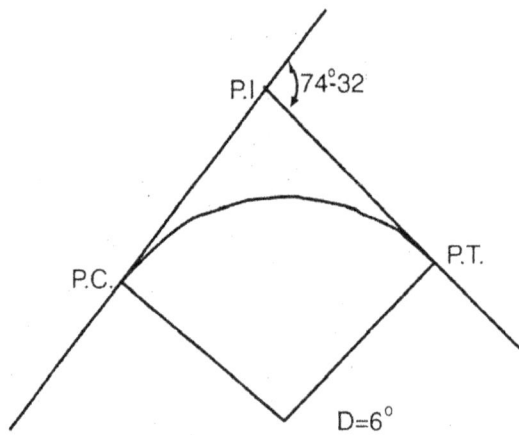

9. The station of the P.C. is 17+57.2.   9._____
   The deflection angle from the P.C. to Sta. 19 is MOST NEARLY

   A. 2°39'   B. 3°17'   C. 4°17'   D. 6°17'

10. The radius of the curve is, in feet, MOST NEARLY   10._____

    A. 955   B. 960   C. 970   D. 980

11. The station of the P.T. is MOST NEARLY   11._____

    A. 29+99.2   B. 29+99.4   C. 29+99.6   D. 30+00.4

12. Two cylindrical tanks with vertical axes lie one above the other. The lower tank is 8'0" in diameter and 8'0" high. The upper tank is 4'0" in diameter and 40'0" high with its base at the level of the top of the lower tank. The lower tank is full of water, and the upper tank is empty.   12._____
    The energy, in foot-pounds, required to pump the water from the lower to the upper tank is MOST NEARLY

    A. 502,000   B. 505,000   C. 508,000   D. 511,000

Questions 13-18.

DIRECTIONS: Questions 13 through 18 refer to the sketch of the plate girder shown below.

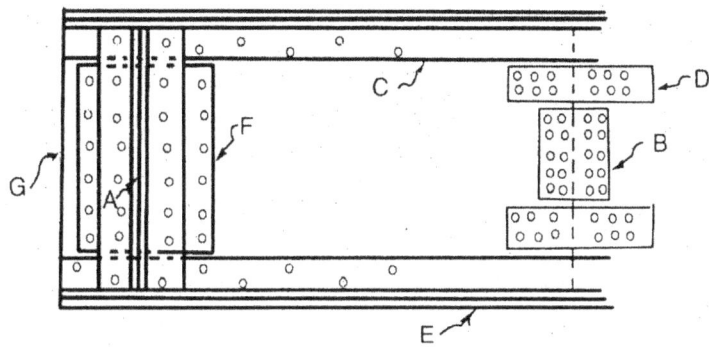

For each of the parts of the plate girder listed below in Questions 13 through 18, select the letter representing that part in the sketch above. For each of questions 13 through 18, the correct answer is

A. A   B. B   C. C   D. D   E. E   F. F   G. G

13. Flange angle   13._____

14. Shear splice   14._____

15. Stiffener   15._____

16. Cover plate   16._____

17. Web   17._____

18. Filler plate   18._____

19. Of the following symbols, the one that represents the ratio of the modulus of elasticity of steel to the modulus of elasticity of concrete in concrete design is   19._____

     A. k   B. v   C. p   D. n

20. A rectangular gate 4'0" wide by 6'0" high is submerged in water with the 4'0" side parallel to and 2'0" below the water surface. The gate is in a vertical plane.
The total pressure on the gate is, in pounds, MOST NEARLY   20._____

     A. 7480   B. 7590   C. 7660   D. 7720

21. The distance from the top of the gate to the center of pressure of the water on one side of the gate described in the preceding question is, in feet, MOST NEARLY   21._____

     A. 3.60   B. 3.70   C. 3.80   D. 3.90

22. Reservoir A is connected to Reservoir B by two parallel pipes, one 6 inches in diameter, the other 12 inches in diameter. The friction factor, f, is the same for each pipe.
If the flow in the 12-inch pipe is 6 cubic feet per second, the flow in the 6-inch pipe is, in cubic feet per second, MOST NEARLY   22._____

     A. 1.01   B. 1.03   C. 1.05   D. 1.06

23. The hydraulic radius of a rectangular channel 6'0" wide with, a 4'0" depth of water is, in feet, MOST NEARLY   23._____

4 (#3)

A. 1.71   B. 1.75   C. 1.79   D. 1.83

24. On a transit, the tangent screw is used to

     A. clamp the telescope in either erect or inverted position
     B. adjust the level bubbles
     C. focus the objective lens
     D. rotate the telescope small distances

25. The tangent of angle A is equal to

     A. $\sqrt{1-\cos^2 A}$ B. $\dfrac{\sec A}{\cos A}$ C. $\sin A \cos A$ D. $\dfrac{\sin A}{\cos A}$

26. If two stations on a mass diagram for earthwork have equal ordinates, the

     A. elevations of the two stations are the same
     B. end areas at the two stations are equal
     C. volume of cut equals the volume of fill between the two stations
     D. volume of fill between the two stations may be moved with equal economy to either station

27. The primary cause of parallax in a telescope is

     A. atmospheric disturbances
     B. maladjustment of the cross hairs
     C. improper focusing of the objective
     D. improper focusing of the eyepiece

28. The notes for a three level section for a roadway 20 ft. wide are as follows:

$$\dfrac{c12}{16} \quad \dfrac{c13}{0} \quad \dfrac{c16}{18}$$

The side slopes of the embankment are _____ horizontal to _____ vertical.
     A. 1; 2   B. 1; 1   C. 2; 1   D. 2; 3

29. Various combinations of the known parts of a triangle are given below. The combination which does NOT describe a unique triangle (i.e., one triangle and one only) is

     A. three sides
     B. two sides and the included angle
     C. one side and two angles
     D. two sides and an acute angle opposite one of the sides

30. To permit easier operation of vehicles, a tangent is MOST frequently connected to a horizontal circular curve by means of a

     A. reversed curve   B. spiral
     C. parabola   D. hyperbola

31. An alidade is MOST commonly used in conjunction with a

     A. transit   B. plane table
     C. barometer   D. tide gauge

32. The increase in length of a 100-foot stool tape due to a temperature rise of 15°F is, in feet, MOST NEARLY 32.____

A. 0.0001 B. 0.0005 C. 0.01 D. 0.05

33. An instrument used to measure the area of a closed traverse, plotted to scale, is a 33.____

A. integraph
B. clinometer
C. planimeter
D. pantograph

Questions 34-35.

DIRECTIONS: Questions 34 and 35 refer to the following diagrams on the following page.

(Diagram for question 34.)

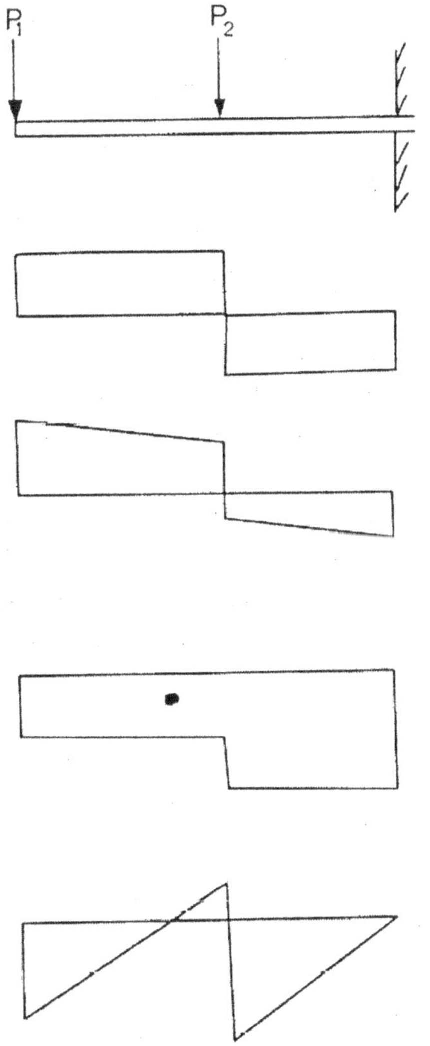

A
B
C
D

(Diagram for question 35.)

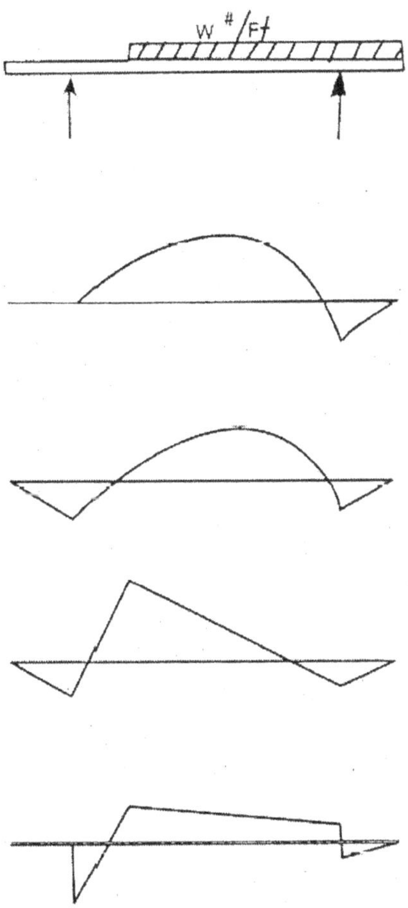

A
B
C
D

34. The shear diagram for the beam shown in the above diagram is (neglecting the weight of the beam) 34.____

A. A B. B C. C D. D

35. The moment diagram for the beam shown in the above diagram is (neglecting the weight of the beam) 35.____

   A. A   B. B   C. C   D. D

Questions 36-40.

DIRECTIONS: In Questions 36 through 40, the plan and front elevation of an object are shown on the left, and on the right are shown four figures, one of which, and only one, represents the right side elevation. Print in the space at the right the letter which represents the right side elevation. In the sample shown below, which figure correctly represents the right side elevation?

     A. A   B. B   C. C   D. D

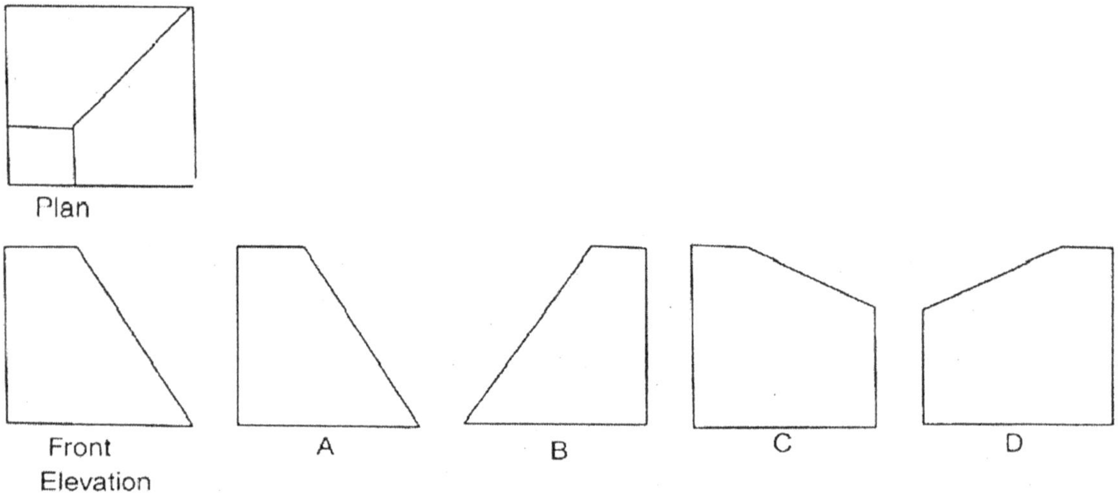

The correct answer is A.

In Questions 36 through 40, which figure correctly represents the right side elevation?

     A. A   B. B   C. C   D. D

36.   36.____

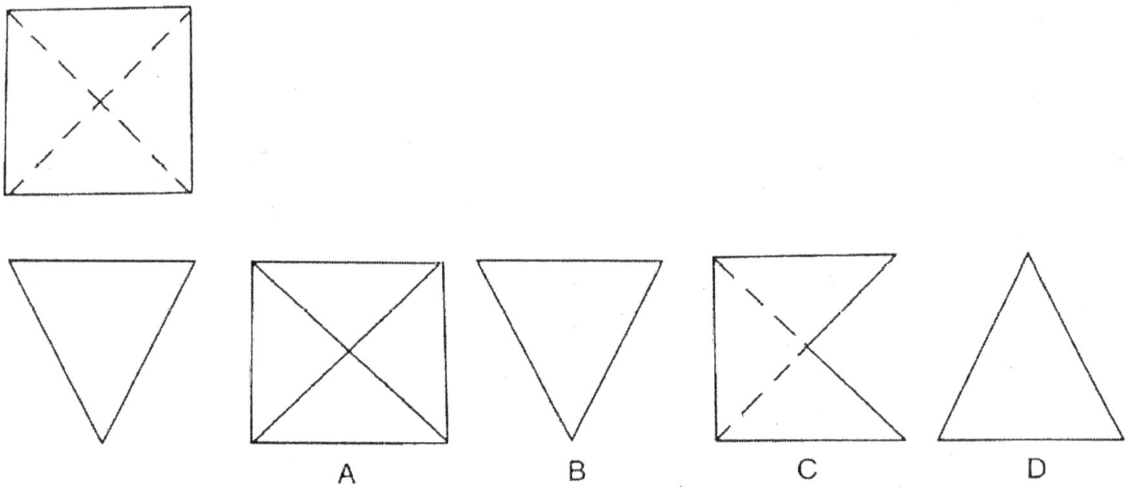

37. Questions 37-40.   37._____

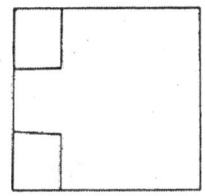

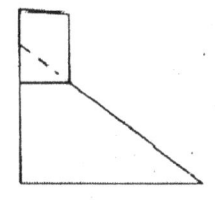 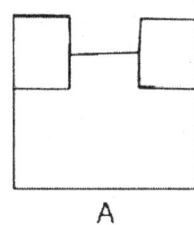 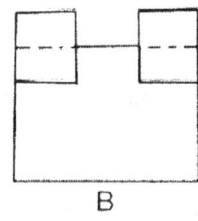 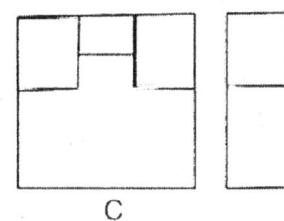 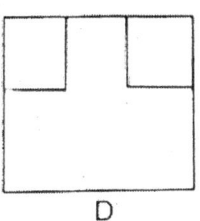
　　　　　　　　A　　　　　　B　　　　　　C　　　　　　D

38.   38._____

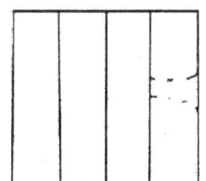

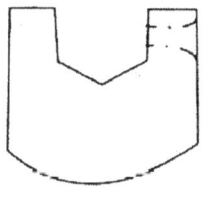 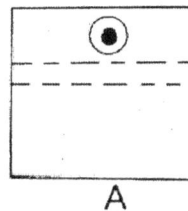 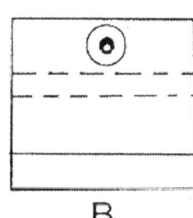 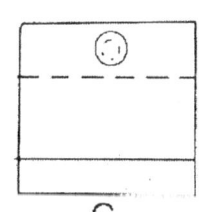 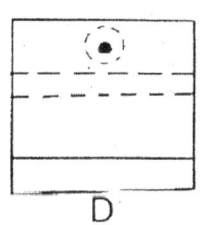
　　　　　　　　A　　　　　　B　　　　　　C　　　　　　D

39.   39._____

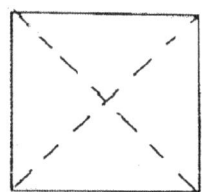

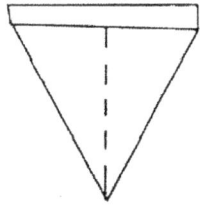 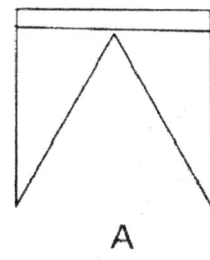 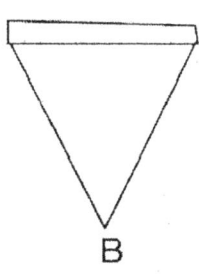 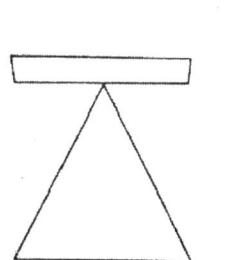 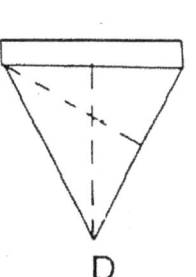
　　　　　　　A　　　　　　B　　　　　　C　　　　　　D

40.   40.____

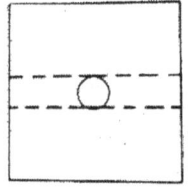

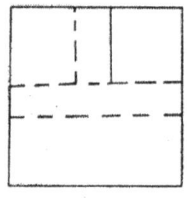 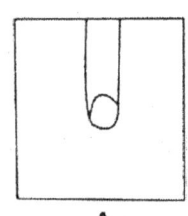 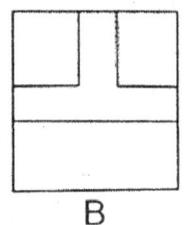 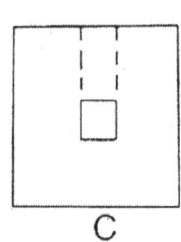 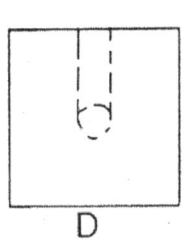
         A   B   C   D

KEY (CORRECT ANSWERS)

1.	A	11.	B	21.	A	31.	B
2.	D	12.	A	22.	D	32.	C
3.	B	13.	C	23.	A	33.	C
4.	A	14.	B	24.	D	34.	C
5.	C	15.	A	25.	D	35.	A
6.	D	16.	E	26.	C	36.	B
7.	A	17.	G	27.	D	37.	A
8.	B	18.	F	28.	A	38.	B
9.	C	19.	D	29.	D	39.	A
10.	A	20.	A	30.	B	40.	C

EXAMINATION SECTION
TEST 1

DIRECTIONS: Each question or incomplete statement is followed by several suggested answers or completions. Select the one that BEST answers the question or completes the statement. *PRINT THE LETTER OF THE CORRECT ANSWER IN THE SPACE AT THE RIGHT.*

1. In pipe laying, the required width of trench in sand is less than that in clay because 1.____

    A. of the dilatancy of the sand
    B. the sand gives the pipe a more uniform support
    C. sand backfill puts less load upon the pipe
    D. of backfilling requirements
    E. it is easier to enlarge the trench for bell holes in sand

2. A short post, 12 inches in diameter, is subjected to 75K applied 1" from the center. The maximum stress in the post, in lbs./sq.in., is MOST NEARLY 2.____

    A. 290   B. 995   C. 1,100   D. 1,260   E. 1,340

3. Of the following, the geological feature which will have the LEAST effect on a foundation is 3.____

    A. stratification   B. foliation or cleavage
    C. striation   D. dip and strike
    E. faults

4. In tall steel frame buildings, the columns are usually erected in lengths of 4.____

    A. 16 feet   B. 20 feet
    C. one story   D. two stories
    E. three stories

5. The P.C. of a 7° curve is at Sta. 16+25.0. The deflection angle to Sta. 17+00 is 5.____

    A. 4° 29'   B. 3° 18'   C. 2° 38'   D. 1° 97'   E. 0° 42'

6. Reverse curves on highways are customarily separated by tangents. Of the following, the BEST reason for this separation is 6.____

    A. to increase sight-distance
    B. to increase the radii of the curves
    C. to improve the appearance of the highway
    D. to avoid sudden changes in curvature
    E. concerned with superelevation

7. The modulus of rupture of a wooden beam is 7.____

    A. greater than the ultimate strength in tension
    B. less than the ultimate strength in tension
    C. a function of the shearing strength if the beam is long
    D. less than the ultimate strength in compression
    E. independent of the cross-section of the beam

8. Plain sedimentation is usually preferred to chemical precipitation in sewage treatment because 8.____

   A. disposition of the sludge resulting from chemical precipitation is difficult
   B. it removes a greater percentage of total suspended matter
   C. it removes a greater percentage of organic matter
   D. chemical precipitation always increases the pH concentration
   E. the resulting sludge is not putrescible

9. The strength of clay sewer pipe is NOT usually determined by a(n) _____ test. 9.____

   A. two-edge bearing
   B. three-edge bearing
   C. sand bearing
   D. *knife-edge*
   E. Izod or impact

10. The maximum moment that three moving loads of 6, 8, and 10 kips, from left to right, respectively, spaced 6 feet apart, can cause on a span of 30 feet is, in K feet, 10.____

    A. 110   B. 120.4   C. G. 152.6   D. 132.2   E. 95.1

11. In stream flow, a curve of rate of discharge versus gage height is known as a 11.____

    A. rating curve
    B. mass diagram
    C. Rippl diagram
    D. flood curve
    E. calibration curve

12. An inverted syphon carries a canal from one side of a valley at Elev. 100 to the other at Elev. 95. Assuming the coefficient of pipe friction is independent of diameter, the required diameter of pipe varies as 12.____

    A. $Q^{9/10}$ B. $Q^{4/5}$ C. $Q^{3/5}$ D. $Q^{2/5}$ E. $Q^{1/5}$

13. Two pipe lines carrying water are at the same elevation. Each is connected to a Bourdon Gage, the center of which is 4 feet vertically above the pipe center.
    If one gage registers 10 feet and the other minus 2 feet, the difference in pressure between the two pipes, in pounds per square inch, is about 13.____

    A. 6.9   B. 6.7   C. 5.9   D. 4.7   E. 3.9

14. The reason wooden beams bearing on brick walls are cut at the end with a mitre is 14.____

    A. a precaution in the event of fire
    B. so the inspector can be sure the beam is well seated
    C. to expose a fresh surface so that faulty wood may be detected
    D. that beams so cut may be placed more easily
    E. to make fire-stopping easier

15. Of the following conditions, shearing stress in the web of rolled steel beams is MOST likely to influence the choice of section when 15.____

    A. headroom requires the use of a section shallower than the most economical section
    B. the span is long and carries several uniformly spaced concentrated loads
    C. the deflection is small
    D. the span is long and carries two heavy concentrated loads, one near each support
    E. the span is long and uniformly loaded

16. The gridiron system of water distribution is

    A. preferable to the branching system with regard to fire protection
    B. only used in the largest cities
    C. less advantageous than the branching system because it requires a superimposed high pressure system
    D. being replaced by the branching system
    E. impractical in developments with many curved streets

17. An advantage of reinforced concrete beam and girder construction, as compared to flat slab construction, is

    A. greater fire resistance
    B. cheaper form work
    C. sprinkler layout is easier
    D. ventilation of rooms is easier
    E. none of the above

18. Activated sludge is sludge that

    A. is mixed mechanically
    B. has been *seeded*
    C. is stirred by air currents which give it a spiral motion
    D. is agitated in any one of several ways
    E. has been removed from a drying bed

19. In water purification, *aeration* is used to remove

    A. turbidity   B. dissolved oxygen
    C. sediment   D. organic material
    E. objectionable gases

20. The maximum unit stress to which a material may be subjected without suffering permanent deformation is known as the

    A. elastic limit   B. yield strength
    C. proportional limit   D. yield point
    E. commercial elastic limit

21. The distance in inches from the back of the short leg to the center of gravity of a 5" x 4" x 1/2" steel angle is APPROXIMATELY

    A. 0.80   B. 1.15   C. 1.40   D. 1.55   E. 1.60

22. A symmetrical triangular roof truss of four panels at 10 feet having a span of 40 feet between end supports and a rise of 10 feet carries a vertical load at the top center of 20,000 pounds.
    The stress in the upper chord of the end panel, in pounds, is APPROXIMATELY

    A. 15,500   B. 19,500   C. 22,500   D. 26,500   E. 28,500

23. A short concrete column with an effective cross-section 30 inches square has two percent vertical steel reinforcing with proper tie.
    Assuming f_c = 500 pounds per square inch, n = 15, the live load that can safely be carried by this column is
    MOST NEARLY _____ pounds.

    A. 550,000   B. 575,000   C. 650,000   D. 675,000   E. 700,000

24. A welded cylindrical horizontal steel tank 36 inches in diameter is subjected to an internal pressure caused by 72-foot head of water. The ends of the tank are capped with hemispherical heads extending outward.
If the allowable tensile strength of the steel be taken as 18,000 lbs. per sq. in., the theoretical thickness of the heads should be, in inches,

    A. 0.735   B. 0.015   C. 0.475   D. 0.625   E. 0.375

25. Water flows from reservoir A, elev. 178, to reservoir B, elev. 106, through 3220 feet of 6" pipe; f = .02.
The velocity in the pipe, in ft./sec., is MOST NEARLY

    A. 1   B. 2   C. 3.5   D. 4.5   E. 6

26. Water is flowing through an open channel of triangular cross-section. The side slopes of the channel are 1:1. The water is 8 feet deep.
The hydraulic radius is

    A. 7.65   B. 6.40   C. 4.37   D. 3.59   E. 2.82

27. The building code of the large city specifies that bearing piles of wood shall not be spaced closer center to center, in inches, than

    A. 20   B. 24   C. 28   D. 32   E. 36

28. The four sides of a rectangular pier have a uniform batter of 2 inches per foot.
If the top of the pier is 4 feet by 10 feet and the pier is 12 feet high, the volume, to the NEAREST cubic foot, is

    A. 668   B. 880   C. 992   D. 745   E. 858

29. To lay out a line 170.00 feet long with a 100-foot tape which is actually 100.03 feet long, the taped distance should be

    A. 169.03   B. 169.95   C. 170.45   D. 170.50   E. 170.65

30. Of the following, the LEAST satisfactory method of preventing electrolysis in underground pipe lines near street railways is

    A. applying an insulating coat to the pipe
    B. using track joint bonds
    C. using track joint bonds and cross bonds
    D. using insulating joints on the pipe
    E. providing drains for the road bed

31. A uniformly loaded beam is continuous over four uniformly spaced supports, A, B, C, and D, reading from left to right.
If the support B settles slightly, the

    A. reaction at D decreases   B. reaction at C decreases
    C. moment at C decreases   D. moment at B increases
    E. reaction at A decreases

32. A flanged shaft coupling uses four 1-inch bolts equispaced on a circle 6 inches in radius. 32.____
    When the shaft is transmitting 300 horsepower at 200 r.p.m., the stress in the bolts, in
    pounds per square inch, is MOST NEARLY

    A. 5000   B. 4500   C. 4000   D. 3500   E. 3000

33. A simple beam on a 16 foot span carries a concentrated load of 5000 pounds at the mid- 33.____
    point.
    If E is 1,600,000 pounds per square inch and I is 1728 inches fourth, the center deflec-
    tion, in inches, is MOST NEARLY

    A. 0.27   B. 0.39   C. 0.47   D. 0.59   E. 0.67

34. The tensile efficiency of a riveted butt joint with adequate straps is a function of 34.____

    A. rivet diameter and plate width
    B. rivet diameter and plate thickness
    C. rivet diameter, plate width, and plate thickness
    D. plate width and thickness
    E. rivet value in double shear and in bearing

35. A 24-inch beam is made up of two 12-inch steel I-beams, the flanges in contact being riv- 35.____
    eted.
    If the moment of inertia of a single 12-inch beam is 300 inches fourth and the cross-
    sectional area 15 square inches, the moment of inertia of the 24-inch beam is, in
    inches fourth, MOST NEARLY

    A. 2390   B. 1680   C. 1540   D. 920   E. 580

36. A distance taped on a 3 percent slope is 231.24 feet. The length, in feet, of the horizontal 36.____
    projection is

    A. 231.14   B. 231.07   C. 231.00   D. 230.93   E. 230.86

37. In running a closed level circuit, 50 set-ups were made. If each of the rod readings varied 37.____
    accidentally by plus or minus 0.003 feet from its correct value, the probable error of clo-
    sure of the circuit is, in feet,

    A. 0.405   B. 0.325   C. 0.030   D. 0.015   E. 0.005

38. The dry weight of a cubic foot of sand is 104 pounds. The specific gravity of the sand 38.____
    grains is 2.60.
    The submerged weight of a cubic foot of this sand in fresh water is, in pounds,

    A. 56   B. 60   C. 64   D. 68   E. 72

39. A street 40 feet wide with a parabolic cross-section has a crown of 6 inches at the center. 39.____
    The elevation of a point on the street surface 4 feet from the gutter is below the crown
    a distance, in inches, of

    A. 1.29   B. 2.73   C. 3.84   D. 4.51   E. 5.19

40. Line AB is extended to C with the transit set at A, a single, careful sight being taken. Subsequently, the transit is set at B, and C checked by a *double reverse*. All three points are at the same elevation.
If C fails to check the average of the *double reverse,* the transit is not in adjustment in that

   A. the horizontal axis is not perpendicular to the vertical axis
   B. the line of sight is not perpendicular to the horizontal axis
   C. either *a* or *b* or both may be the cause
   D. the axis of the objective slide does not coincide with the optical axis
   E. the line of sight is not parallel to the long bubble

41. The BEST material to use for a hydraulic-fill dam is a well-graded mixture ranging from

   A. gravel to fine silt
   B. sand to clay
   C. coarse sand to silt
   D. gravel to fine sand
   E. chips to ash

42. A round steel bar, one inch in diameter, is embedded 40 inches in concrete.
The unit tensile stress in the bar which will develop a bond stress of 100 pounds per square inch is, in pounds per square inch, about

   A. 19,000   B. 17,000   C. 16,000   D. 15,000   E. 13,000

43. The MOST important advantage of the Invar tape over the ordinary steel tape is it(s)

   A. will not rust
   B. high modulus of elasticity
   C. low coefficient of thermal expansion
   D. greater strength
   E. cheapness

44. Two clean steel pipes, one 12 inches in diameter, the other 6 inches in diameter, run from one reservoir to another in parallel.
If the slope of the hydraulic gradient is the same for the two pipes, the ratio of the discharge of the larger pipe to that of the smaller is about

   A. 5.6   B. 4.7   C. 3.9   D. 2.3   E. 1.1

45. The use of steel pipe to convey water is desirable because it

   A. never requires an inside coating
   B. can be fabricated by unskilled labor
   C. is not subject to electrolysis
   D. can carry large external loads
   E. does not have to be caulked

46. Reinforcing steel is usually shaped on the job

   A. by heating in a forge
   B. by cutting and welding
   C. by hand bending
   D. never
   E. on a bar-bending table

47. *Bulking* of sand

    A. is a maximum with a water content of about 6%
    B. is of no importance in concrete proportioning
    C. varies directly as the moisture content
    D. is greater for a coarse sand than a fine sand
    E. does not occur unless the sand contains over one-half gallon of water per cubic foot

48. The cinders used in *cinder concrete* should be

    A. thoroughly wetted down at least 24 hours before mixing
    B. thoroughly dry before mixing
    C. fine and powdery
    D. at least 50 percent uncombined carbon
    E. at least 50 percent combined carbon

49. Bank-run gravel ordinarily

    A. contains no sand
    B. contains too much sand to make a well-proportioned aggregate for concrete
    C. makes a well-proportioned aggregate for concrete
    D. contains too little sand to make a well-proportioned aggregate for concrete
    E. makes a good binder for macadam roads

50. The practical limit on the depth below water level to which the pneumatic caisson process may be carried is, in feet,

    A. 75   B. 85   C. 95   D. 110   E. 125

KEY (CORRECT ANSWERS)

1. D	11. A	21. D	31. A	41. B
2. C	12. D	22. C	32. A	42. C
3. C	13. A	23. B	33. A	43. C
4. D	14. A	24. B	34. A	44. A
5. C	15. D	25. E	35. B	45. E
6. E	16. A	26. E	36. A	46. E
7. A	17. E	27. B	37. C	47. A
8. A	18. B	28. B	38. C	48. A
9. E	19. E	29. B	39. C	49. B
10. D	20. A	30. A	40. D	50. D

TEST 2

DIRECTIONS: Each question or incomplete statement is followed by several suggested answers or completions. Select the one that BEST answers the question or completes the statement. *PRINT THE LETTER OF THE CORRECT ANSWER IN THE SPACE AT THE RIGHT.*

1. In earthwork, if two stations on a mass diagram have equal ordinates of like sign

    A. between the two stations, the volume of cut equals the volume of fill
    B. elevation of surface at the two stations is the same
    C. depth of cut or fill at the two stations is the same
    D. the distance between two stations equals the limit of economical haul

2. In the design of a reinforced concrete footing, which carries a reinforced concrete column, the distance from the face of the column to the critical section for shear is, in inches,

    A. kd   B. jd   C. d   D. zero

3. A major city building code permits reduction in the design live load of columns below the top floor as computed on the basis of design floor load because

    A. loads on lower floors offset moments created by loads on upper floors
    B. side sway is less when all floors are fully loaded
    C. lower columns are better braced
    D. it is unreasonable to expect all floors to be fully loaded at the same time

4. The term S2S means _____ two sides.

    A. shellac   B. sandpaper
    C. surfaced   D. split

5. The term *drop panel* is commonly used in

    A. plastering walls   B. plywood forms
    C. prefabricated housing   D. flat slab construction

6. In controlled concrete, the water-cement ratio is selected on the basis of

    A. consistency desired   B. proportion of aggregates
    C. type of aggregates   D. strength desired

7. A surcharge is usually MOST closely associated with

    A. highway superelevation   B. very long piles
    C. allowable fluid pressure D. retaining walls

8. Steam at 300 lb./sq.in. flows through a 1 ft. diameter pipe. The pipe walls are 1 in. thick. The unit circumferential stress is, in pounds per square inch,

    A. 900   B. 1800   C. 3200   D. 4800

9. On a topographic map, the symbol shown at the right represents
    A. tidal flat
    B. cultivated land
    C. orchard
    D. salt marsh

10. A square steel plate, 8 ft. on a side, is submerged in water with the top edge parallel to the water surface and 10 ft. below the surface.
    If the plate makes an angle of 30 with the water surface, the total pressure on the plate is, in pounds,

    A. 2688   B. 8649   C. 31,560   D. 47,900

    10.____

11. The stress in a steel bar 8 feet long, cross-sectional area 4 sq.in., rigidly set in a wall at both ends, due to a temperature rise of 30° F is, in pounds per square inch, (E = 30 x 10^6 lb./sq.in.; coefficient of expansion = 645 x 10^{-8})

    A. 628   B. 2775   C. 5800   D. 12,235

    11.____

12. The maximum unit stress up to which a material may be stressed without suffering permanent deformation when the stress is removed is called

    A. proportional limit   B. yield point
    C. elastic limit   D. ultimate stress

    12.____

13. The elongation of a steel bar, 100 feet long, cross-sectional area 1 sq.in., supported at one end and hanging vertically, due to its own weight is, in inches,
    (Steel weighs 490 lb./cu.ft.; E = 30 x 10^6 lb./sq.in.)

    A. .0019   B. .0068   C. .0077   D. .1586

    13.____

14. Lehoann's solution is used to determine

    A. orientation of a plane table
    B. longitude of station
    C. elevation of B.M. by method of least squares
    D. distances in a triangulation net

    14.____

15. In laying out a circular curve, the formula $R \text{ vers} \frac{1}{2} I$ is used to determine the

    A. middle ordinate   B. tangent distance
    C. long chord   D. external distance

    15.____

16. The results of a survey of a closed traverse are as follows:

Line	Lat.	Dep.
AB	100.62	272.21
BC	153.27	422.16
CD	-322.14	19.23
DA	68.33	-713.50

    The magnitude of the linear error of closure is, in feet,

    A. .04   B. .07   C. .13   D. .15

    16.____

17. The notes for a three level section for a 20 feet wide roadway are

    $\frac{c\,7.5}{15} \quad \frac{c\,9}{0} \quad \frac{c\,12}{18}$

    The cross-sectional area of cut is, in square feet,

    A. 198   B. 246   C. 327   D. 415

    17.____

18. To determine the elevation of a point on the face of a building, a level was set up, a sight of 1.487 taken with a rod on the cap bolt of a hydrant, Elev. 39.470, and another sight taken on a tape with its zero end at the point (the tape stretching downward from the point).
If the reading on the tape was 1.212, the elevation of the point is

   A. 42.169   B. 41.353   C. 40.457   D. 39.899

19. In taping, an accidental error may result from

   A. the tapeman unintentionally making a mistake
   B. the temperature being greater than that at which tape was standardized
   C. causes beyond control of the tapeman
   D. assuming slope distances to be horizontal distances

20. The maximum shearing stress in a wood joist 3 in. by 10 in., actual dimensions, simply supported at its ends on a 14 feet span, and sustaining a uniform load, including its own weight of 150 lb./ft. over the entire length is, in pounds per square inch,

   A. 39   B. 52   C. 68   D. 126

21. If the moment of inertia of a section is 1500 in. 4, and its area is 12 sq.in., the radius of gyration of the section is, in inches, APPROXIMATELY

   A. 11   B. 27   C. 49   D. 101

22. Of the following types of wall, which one is LEAST like the others in function? _____ wall.

   A. Curtain   B. Retaining   C. Spandrel   D. Wing

23. The bending moment at the ends of a beam rigidly supported at both ends and carrying a uniform load of w #/ft. throughout its entire length 1 ft. is, in ft.lbs.,

   A. $\dfrac{w1^2}{8}$ B. $\dfrac{w1}{10}$ C. $\dfrac{w1^2}{10}$ D. $\dfrac{w1^2}{12}$

24. The hydraulic radius of a rectangular canal 4 feet wide is 1.20.
The depth of flow, in feet, is

   A. 1.6   B. 2.1   C. 2.6   D. 3.0

25. The dynamic pressure into which the kinetic energy of water is transformed when the valve at the outlet of a pipe is suddenly closed is called

   A. velocity head   B. static head
   C. water hammer   D. hydraulic gradient

26. The length of a 3/8" fillet weld required to resist a shear of 12,000 lbs., if the allowable shearing stress is 13,000 lb./sq.in., is, in inches,

   A. 1.97   B. 2.31   C. 2.77   D. 3.48

27. Bridge trusses are built with a slight camber in order to   27.___

    A. make erection easier
    B. avoid sag under load
    C. eliminate secondary stresses
    D. reduce tension in lower chord

28. The formula for determining the value of *n* in concrete design, as given by the A.C.I. and   28.___
    a major city building code is

    A. $\dfrac{3000}{f'c}$ B. $\dfrac{fs}{f'c}$ C. $\dfrac{fs}{fc}$ D. $\dfrac{Es}{fcX10^3}$

29. In reinforced concrete design with fs = 18,000 lb./sq.in., fc = 1000 lb./sq.in. and n = 12,   29.___
    the value of k is

    A. .389   B. .396   C. .400   D. .420

30. Water flows through a 2" ⌀ orifice in the side of a tank under a head of 20 ft.   30.___
    If Cd = .60, the quantity of discharge is, in cfs,

    A. .47   B. .91   C. 1.27   D. 239.4

31. Water discharges through a turbine at the rate of 60,000 cfm under a head of 100 ft.   31.___
    If the efficiency of the turbine is 70%, the horsepower developed by the turbine is

    A. 646   B. 7,950   C. 21,300   D. 44,440

32. Stirrups are used in concrete construction to   32.___

    A. support reinforcing rods
    B. reinforce concrete for the diagonal tension component of shear
    C. hold forms together
    D. prevent cracking of concrete due to changes of temperature

33. In the design of a steel member in tension, rivet holes must be deducted to obtain the net   33.___
    section.
    This is not done when the member is in compression because

    A. rivet holes are smaller
    B. formulae for design of compression members reduce allowable stress
    C. rivets can be placed more efficiently
    D. rivets are assumed to fill the holes

34. In a specific gravity determination, the weight of a flask full of water is 390.0 grams. The   34.___
    weight of the same flask filled with water and 96.2 grams of sand is 450.0 grams. The
    specific gravity of the sand is

    A. 2.58   B. 2.66   C. 2.74   D. 2.82

35. A soil has a void ratio of 0.80 and a specific gravity of solids of 2.67.   35.___
    The total weight (including the water) of a saturated cubic foot of this soil is, in pounds,

    A. 173.4   B. 120.4   C. 111.1   D. 72.7

36. The loss in head per 1,000 feet in a 12-inch water pipe is 9 feet, and the friction factor, f, is 0.0161.
    The velocity of flow in the pipe is, in feet per second,

    A. 6.0   B. 8.1   C. 13.9   D. 18.3

Questions 37-40.

DIRECTIONS: Questions 37 through 40 refer to the truss shown below.

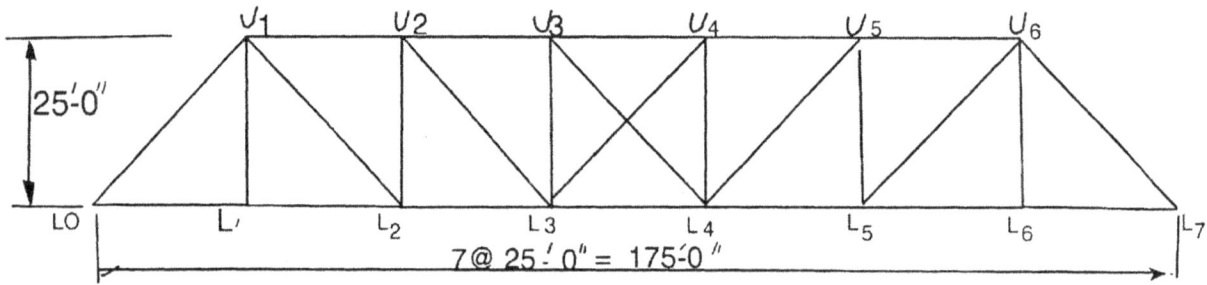

37. If a uniformly distributed live load of 2 kips per foot extends over the entire length of the truss, the live load shear in panel L_2L_3 is, in kips,

    A. 150   B. 100   C. 50   D. 0

38. If the stress in U_2L_2 is -150 kips (compression) and in L_1L_2 +300 kips (tension), the stress in L_2L_3 is, in kips,

    A. +619   B. +450   C. +324   D. +108

39. For a uniformly distributed live load, the maximum tensile stress in member U_2L_3 will occur when the truss is loaded from the

    A. right up to panel point L_3
    B. right up to a point between L_3 and L_2
    C. left up to panel point L_2
    D. left up to a point between L_2 and L_3

40. For a uniformly distributed live load, the maximum tensile stress in member U_2L_2 will occur when the truss is loaded from the left up to

    A. panel point L_3
    B. panel point L_2
    C. a point midway between L_2 and L_3
    D. a point 8'4" from L_2 in panel L_2L_3

KEY (CORRECT ANSWERS)

1. A	11. C	21. A	31. B
2. C	12. C	22. A	32. B
3. D	13. B	23. D	33. D
4. C	14. A	24. D	34. B
5. D	15. A	25. C	35. B
6. D	16. C	26. D	36. A
7. D	17. B	27. B	37. C
8. B	18. A	28. A	38. B
9. D	19. C	29. C	39. B
10. D	20. B	30. A	40. D

TEST 3

DIRECTIONS: Each question or incomplete statement is followed by several suggested answers or completions. Select the one that BEST answers the question or completes the statement. *PRINT THE LETTER OF THE CORRECT ANSWER IN THE SPACE AT THE RIGHT.*

1. A grit chamber is an enlarged channel through which sewage flows

    A. while being screened
    B. with a velocity of from 0.6 to 2.6 feet per minute
    C. with a velocity reduced to cause heavy solids to be deposited
    D. depositing grit which decomposes in the bottom
    E. in recessed chambers

2. An end post is

    A. a long column
    B. a diagonal compression member
    C. a short column
    D. the end member of a compression chord on a through truss
    E. the outside vertical member of a bent

3. A strut is

    A. a long column
    B. a diagonal compression member
    C. a wide column
    D. the end member of a compression chord on a through truss
    E. the outside vertical member of a bent

4. Of the following items, the one which has NOTHING to do with stadia computations is

    A. Cox computer   B. Beaman arc
    C. stadia slide rule   D. stadia tables
    E. gradienter

5. In laying up a brick wall, bond refers to the

    A. adhesive property of the mortar
    B. anchors or ties which hold a brick veneer wall to a building
    C. beam anchors
    D. use of bats or half bricks
    E. use of headers and stretchers

6. In a reinforced concrete building of the slab beam and girder type, architectural considerations limit the size of one beam to such an extent that the concrete stress in that beam is excessive.
   The MOST practical solution is to

    A. ignore the architectural considerations
    B. use a better quality concrete throughout the building
    C. use a better quality concrete in the beam under consideration
    D. increase the required tension steel
    E. provide compression steel

7. A reinforced concrete beam 10" wide x 12" effective depth, on a simple span of 12'0", is reinforced in tension only with three 1/2" square rods.
If the allowable steel and concrete stresses are 18,000 and 600 p.s.i., respectively, and K is 1/3, the maximum uniform load that the beam can carry (including its own weight) is, in pounds per foot,

 A. 592 B. 623 C. 667 D. 689 E. 714

7.____

8. A statically indeterminate structure

 A. is one to which the equations of static equilibrium do not apply
 B. is statically indeterminate because of secondary stresses
 C. requires more material than an equivalent statically determinate structure because of the uncertainty of the exact values of the stresses in the former
 D. is statically indeterminate because of rigid joints
 E. requires at least one equation in addition to those of static equilibrium, for a solution

8.____

9. A masonry wall with a rectangular cross-section is 14 feet high.
If water stands behind the wall two feet below its top and if the masonry weighs 150 pounds per cubic foot, the required width of the wall to just prevent overturning is, in feet,

 A. 4.14 B. 4.54 C. 5.24 D. 5.84 E. 6.04

9.____

10. If the hydraulic radius of a stream is close to unity, the cross-section of the stream is

 A. semi-circular   B. square
 C. triangular   D. deep and narrow
 E. wide and shallow

10.____

11. In column formulae, allowance for accidental eccentricity

 A. is made in the factor of safety
 B. is a function of length
 C. is not made
 D. depends only on the section of the column
 E. must be estimated by the designer

11.____

12. An emergency pipe line connecting two reservoirs consists of 3,000 feet of 16" pipe followed by 6,000 feet of 24" pipe which leads into the lower reservoir.
The hydraulic grade line for this pipe

 A. does not drop continuously in the direction of flow
 B. drops continuously in the direction of flow
 C. is affected by the ground profile
 D. is affected by the pipe profile
 E. never rises in the direction of flow

12.____

13. The use of several pipes rather than one pipe in an inverted syphon carrying a sewer under a subway is considered good practice because

    A. it helps prevent deposition in the syphon
    B. it reduces the headroom required
    C. several small pipes are cheaper than one big one
    D. the resultant head loss is smaller
    E. it reduces the velocity of flow

14. If the objective lens of a transit telescope is focused to give an observer the clearest possible view of an object,

    A. no parallax can exist
    B. the proper way to eliminate parallax would involve refocusing of both objective and eyepiece
    C. parallax should be ignored
    D. any error due to parallax can be eliminated by a direct and a reversed sight
    E. nothing can be done to eliminate any parallax that may exist

15. The ground rod at Sta. 18+00 is 6.2. If the grade rod is 8.8,

    A. the fill is 3.7
    B. the cut is 14.8
    C. the fill is 15.0
    D. there is no way of telling whether there is cut or fill of 14.8
    E. there is no way of telling whether there is cut or fill of 3.7

16. In a circular curve of radius R and central angle I, the distance $R(\frac{1}{\cos \frac{1}{2}} - 1)$ is used to locate the

    A. point of curvature
    B. point of intersection or vertex
    C. center of the curve from the vertex
    D. midpoint of the chord of the circular curve
    E. midpoint of the long chord

17. A line 442.25 feet long is to be laid out with a 100-foot steel tape which is 100.07 feet long.
    The taped length which should be laid out in the field is

    A. 441.94   B. 441.99   C. 442.04   D. 442.09   E. 442.14

18. Water flows from reservoir A, Elev. 100, to reservoir B through 16,100 feet of 12-inch pipe.
    If the friction factor, f, is 0.02 and the flow 3.14 cubic feet per second, the elevation of the water surface in reservoir B is MOST NEARLY

    A. 32   B. 28   C. 24   D. 20   E. 16

19. The area bounded by the X-axis, the ordinates x = 1 and x = 4, and the curve $y = x^2-6x-7$ is

    A. 45   B. 41   C. 37   D. 33   E. 29

20. A tie rod 20'0" long and one inch in diameter, fastened to rigid supports at its ends, is under a tension of 10,000 p.s.i. when the temperature is 68° F.
    If the temperature rises to 98° F, the tension in the rod will be MOST NEARLY, in p.s.i.,

    A. 4140   B. 5960   C. 7235   D. 10,800   E. 13,444

21. A 14 WF 246 section has a cross-sectional area, in square inches, of about

    A. 63.5   B. 72.5   C. 76.5   D. 80.5   E. 84.5

22. A load of lumber consists of 25 pieces 4" x 6" x 15'3". The total F.B.M. is MOST NEARLY

    A. 8160   B. 6640   C. 762   D. 868   E. 2155

23. In concrete work, the slump test

    A. is used to determine time of initial set
    B. may be used as a rough check of the water-cement ratio
    C. could give identical results for two concrete mixes of entirely different water-cement ratios
    D. is used in the field only after the concrete has proper workability
    E. is gradually being replaced by the Vicat apparatus

24. A gusset plate is attached to one flange of an H-section column by four rivets which lie at the corners of a 6" x 8" rectangle with the 6" side horizontal. The plate carries a vertical concentrated load with action line 20 inches to the right of the center of the rivet group. Lettering the rivets a, b, c, and d in clockwise order starting at the upper lefthand corner, the maximum total rivet stress occurs in

    A. a and b   B. b and d   C. b only
    D. b and c   E. c and d

25. A steel I-beam with a section modulus of 120 inches cubed is to carry a uniformly-distributed load including its own weight on a simple span of 12'0". The maximum allowable fibre stress is 16,000 p.s.i.
    Of the following loads, in pounds per foot (including the weight of the beam), the largest load the beam can carry is

    A. 767   B. 2890   C. 8800   D. 19,705   E. 24,664

26. A flat plate carrying a tensile load of 24,000 pounds is to be connected to a gusset plate by means of 5/16" fillet welds.
    If the allowable unit shearing stress on welds is 11,300 p.s.i., the total length of weld required, in inches, is MOST NEARLY

    A. 27.4   B. 17.3   C. 9.6   D. 7.7   E. 6.6

27. The latitudes and departures of a closed traverse are as follows:

Line	Latitude	Departure
AB	+1000	0
BC	0	+1000
CA	-998	-998

    The error of closure is MOST NEARLY

    A. 1:1200   B. 1:1000   C. 1:800   D. 1:500   E. 1:300

28. The flanges and web of an H-section 12" wide by 12" deep are each 1" thick.
    The moment of inertia of the section about an axis through the center of gravity and parallel to the flanges is, in inches fourth,

    A. 263   B. 387   C. 595   D. 811   E. 929

29. A circular gate 4' in diameter lies in a vertical plane with its top 4' below the water surface.
    The total water pressure on one side of the gate, in pounds, is MOST NEARLY

    A. 800   B. 3200   C. 3700   D. 4700   E. 4500

30. Two 3/8" plates under a tension of 50,000 lbs. are lap riveted with 7/8" rivets. Allowable unit values of rivets are 15,000 lbs. p.s.i. for shear and 32,000 lbs. p.s.i. for bearing.
    The number of 7/8" rivets required for this joint is

    A. 1   B. 2   C. 3   D. 4   E. 6

31. A Warren-type deck truss with a span of 60' 0" has 3 panels at 20' 0" and is 20' 0" deep.
    Under a uniform load of one kip per foot per truss, the maximum stress in the compression chord is, in kips,

    A. 40   B. 35   C. 30   D. 20   E. 10

32. The allowable tensile and bond stresses in reinforcing bars for concrete are 16,000 and 100 p.s.i., respectively. The depth of embedment, in inches, required to develop the allowable tensile strength of a 3/4" diameter bar is

    A. 50   B. 30   C. 20   D. 10   E. 5

33. A sedimentation tank is an enlarged channel through which sewage flows

    A. while being screened
    B. with a velocity of from 0.5 to 2.5 feet per minute
    C. with a velocity reduced to cause heavy solids to be deposited
    D. depositing grit which decomposes in the bottom
    E. in recessed chambers

34. A level is set up so that a Philadelphia rod reads 4.00 on B.M.A., elev. 90.00. A tape rod is then set to read 0.00 at B.M.A. and reads 0.84 at point B.
    The elevation of point B is

    A. computed from the H.I.   B. 90.84
    C. 90.37   D. 88.74
    E. 87.14

35. A Proctor compaction test is usually MOST closely associated with the use in the field of a

    A. drag line   B. bulldozer
    C. pile driver   D. sheep's-foot roller
    E. post-hole digger

36. The MOST important consideration in the design of a building foundation resting on a deep clay layer is concerned with

   A. minimum settlement
   B. differential settlement
   C. length of construction period
   D. weather conditions during construction
   E. shape of footing

37. The discharge of a stream varies from 0.1 to 10.0 cubic feet per second, with a mean discharge of about 0.3 c.f.s. The BEST type of weir to measure flow in this stream is

   A. suppressed rectangular
   B. contracted rectangular
   C. trapezoidal
   D. submerged
   E. triangular

38. A peg test on a transit has been completed.
    The first step in the actual adjustment based on the result of the test involves movement of

   A. a diagonally-opposite pair of foot screws
   B. the cross-hair ring
   C. the long bubble by means of the bubble-adjusting screw
   D. the telescope about the horizontal axis
   E. the plate bubbles

39. A steel specimen was tested to destruction in a tension test in which no extensometer was used.
    Results which could be reported would include

   A. elastic limit
   B. yield point
   C. modulus of elasticity
   D. proportional limit
   E. initial set

40. Of the five items following, which one bears the LEAST relationship to the other four?

   A. Shore
   B. Needle
   C. Pretest pile
   D. Underpinning
   E. Pile loading test

KEY (CORRECT ANSWERS)

1. C	11. B	21. B	31. D
2. D	12. A	22. C	32. B
3. B	13. A	23. C	33. B
4. E	14. B	24. D	34. B
5. E	15. C	25. C	35. D
6. E	16. C	26. C	36. B
7. A	17. A	27. A	37. E
8. E	18. D	28. D	38. D
9. A	19. A	29. D	39. B
10. E	20. A	30. E	40. E

EXAMINATION SECTION
TEST 1

DIRECTIONS: Each question or incomplete statement is followed by several suggested answers or completions. Select the one that BEST answers the question or completes the statement. *PRINT THE LETTER OF THE CORRECT ANSWER IN THE SPACE AT THE RIGHT.*

1. For highway design, the radius of a 2 degree curve, in feet, is MOST NEARLY
   A. 2864.8   B. 2854.8   C. 2844.8   D. 2834.8

2. In a typical conventional flexible pavement known as asphalt pavement, the surface course usually consists of two bituminous layers, a wearing course, and a binder course.
   The binder course generally has _____ sized aggregate and a _____ amount of asphalt.
   A. smaller; smaller
   B. larger; smaller
   C. smaller; larger
   D. larger; larger

3. The PRIMARY purpose of a base course on asphalt pavement is to
   A. replace weak soil in the subgrade
   B. distribute the stresses imposed by traffic loading
   C. absorb the impact load imposed by traffic loading
   D. act as an impervious layer of soil to prevent undermining the roadway

4. The traditional material for a base course on an asphalt pavement is
   A. a mixture of sand and gravel with cement as a binder
   B. a mixture of crushed rock with a bituminous emulsion as a binder
   C. crushed stone and natural sand
   D. crushed stone and slag with a small amount of water

5. The AASHO conducted a road test to determine an equivalency factor to convert one pass of any given single or tandem-axle load to equivalent passes of a(n) _____ kip single axle load.
   A. 14   B. 16   C. 18   D. 20

6. Assume the traffic in one lane of a highway increases 4.5% a year.
   If the current traffic is 1,000 cars a day, the daily traffic at the end of 10 years will be MOST NEARLY _____ cars per day.
   A. 1,250   B. 1,350   C. 1,450   D. 1,550

7. The AASHTO set the eye height for determining the minimum stopping sight distance at _____ inches.
   A. 34   B. 39   C. 44   D. 49

8. Vehicle clearances on interstate highways should be a minimum of
   A. 12'6"   B. 13'0"   C. 13'6"   D. 14'0"

9. Where longitudinal drainage on a highway is along the pavement and shoulders, the MINIMUM allowable longitudinal grade is
   A. 0.1%   B. 0.3%   C. 0.5%   D. 0.7%

10. In the specifications section of a highway contract, under *Earthwork* is a paragraph labeled *Clearing and Grubbing*.
    Grubbing refers PRIMARILY to removing
    A. construction debris buried on the site
    B. tree stumps and roots by digging them out
    C. underground structures such as sewers and foundations
    D. topsoil

11. One acre is equal to _____ hectares.
    A. .385   B. .405   C. .425   D. .445

12. A liquid is neutral if its pH value is
    A. 6   B. 7   C. 8   D. 9

13. In the specification section for epoxy-coated reinforcement is the statement, *Chairs, tie wires, and other devices to support, position, or fasten the reinforcement shall be made or coated with a dielectric material.*
    Dielectric in the above statement means it
    A. has the same level of conductivity as the reinforcing bar
    B. does not have an electric field surrounding it
    C. is resistant to corrosion
    D. does not conduct electricity

14. A kiloton is closest to _____ pounds.
    A. 184,000   B. 194,000   C. 214,000   D. 2 million

15. In the specifications for a highway construction project is the item *Force Account Work*.
    This item relates to
    A. work that is required of a contractor caused by his negligence
    B. credit due the owner resulting from a change in the contract provisions
    C. payment for the actual cost of the work performed by the contractor
    D. deduction of payment due to faulty work

16. In a resurvey of the property of Mr. Doe, starting at E and measuring 300 feet, it was discovered that the property of Mr. Doe overlapped the property of Mr. Jones. The shaded area is known as a(n)
    A. incursion   B. recursion   C. gore   D. imposition

17. An absolute estate ownership in property including unlimited power of alienation describes
    A. general warrantee deed B. guarantee title
    C. fee simple   D. dominant land

18. The error, in feet, measuring a distance of 100 feet with a 100 foot tape, with one end of the tape being one foot higher than the other end, will be
    A. .005   B. .006   C. .007   D. .008

19. A 100 foot steel tape will have a change in length of .01 feet with a temperature change, in degrees Fahrenheit, of
    A. 15   B. 18   C. 21   D. 24

20. The effects of the curvature of the earth and refraction on a rod reading in leveling curvature of the earth will _____ the road reading and refraction will _____ the rod reading.
    A. increase; decrease   B. decrease; increase
    C. increase; increase   D. decrease; decrease

21. The North Star is called
    A. Deneb   B. Ursa Minor   C. Ursa Major   D. Polaris

22. One degree is equal, in radians, to
    A. .06981   B. .03490   C. .01745   D. .00873

23. On construction jobs using heavy equipment, the dumpy level is the instrument of choice over the automatic level and laser because of its
    A. accuracy   B. stability
    C. ease of handling   D. magnification power

24. The sum of the interior angles in a closed survey having n sides is _____ 180 degrees.
    A. (n+1)   B. (n)   C. (n-1)   D. (n-2)

25. Gabions are used
    A. to prevent water leakage in soils   B. as a substitute for piles
    C. to build retaining walls   D. to stabilize subgrades

KEY (CORRECT ANSWERS)

1. A
2. B
3. B
4. C
5. C

6. D
7. C
8. D
9. C
10. B

11. B
12. B
13. D
14. D
15. C

16. C
17. C
18. A
19. A
20. A

21. D
22. C
23. B
24. D
25. C

TEST 2

DIRECTIONS: Each question or incomplete statement is followed by several suggested answers or completions. Select the one that BEST answers the question or completes the statement. *PRINT THE LETTER OF THE CORRECT ANSWER IN THE SPACE AT THE RIGHT.*

1. According to OSHA regulations, on a suspension scaffold with a working loaf of 750 pounds, no more than _____ people are permitted on the scaffold.
   A. 2   B. 3   C. 4   D. 5

2. In a table of the capacity of manila rope slings, OSHA uses a factor of safety of
   A. 4   B. 5   C. 6   D. 7

3. Synthetic fiber rope is conventional _____ strand construction.
   A. 2   B. 3   C. 4   D. 5

4. The material for the web of synthetic rope not included in the OSHA regulations is
   A. nylon   B. polyester   C. orlon   D. polypropylene

5. The minimum number and spacing of u-bolt wire rope clips for ½ inch steel rope is _____ clips with a minimum spacing of _____ inches.
   A. 2; 2½   B. 3; 3   C. 3; 3½   D. 3; 4

6. High strength bolts used in slip critical conditions are required to be tightened to a pretension force of about _____% of the minimum tensile stress of the material from which the bolts are made.
   A. 65   B. 70   C. 75   D. 80

7. The tensile force in a bolt used in slip critical conditions can be accomplished by the use of a direct tension indicator.
   The direct tension indicator is a special
   A. bolt   B. nut   C. washer   D. impact wrench

8. The ASTM designation for the commonly used high strength bolts are A325 and
   A. A307   B. A449   C. A490   D. A502

9. The welding process MOST commonly used for manual application is _____ metal arc welding.
   A. shielded   B. gas   C. submerged   D. flux-core

10. Plug and slot welds are used PRIMARILY
    A. for stitching different parts of a member together
    B. when there are heavy shear loads to be transmitted
    C. plates of the same size make the use of fillet welds impractical
    D. where for appearance purposes you don't want the welds to be seen

11. Lamellar tearing in a thick steel plate would MOST likely occur _____ to the direction of rolling.
    A. in a plane perpendicular   B. parallel
    C. perpendicular   D. at 45°

12. In the metric system, the modulus of elasticity of steel is assumed to be _____ GPa.
    A. 100   B. 150   C. 175   D. 200

13. The cross-section area, in square feet, of earth excavated to the roadway bed of a highway is MOST NEARLY
    A. 490   B. 510   C. 530   D. 550

14. The modulus of elasticity of steel may vary from _____ KSI.
    A. 28,000 to 30,000   B. 29,000 to 31,000
    C. 30,000 to 32,000   D. 31,000 to 33,000

15. G in the metric system denotes
    A. 10^3 B. 10^6 C. 10^9 D. 10^{12}

16. A kilonewton, in pounds, is MOST NEARLY
    A. 204   B. 224   C. 244   D. 264

17. Steel weighs 490 pounds per cubic foot. In the metric system, its weight, in kg/m³, is assumed to be
    A. 7350   B. 7550   C. 7650   D. 7850

18. In calculations, a bag of cement is assumed to weigh _____ pounds.
    A. 94   B. 96   C. 98   D. 100

19. The slump range for general purpose structural concrete, in millimeters, is
    A. 40-55   B. 55-70   C. 70-85   D. 85-100

20. The concrete mix with the HIGHEST slump would be used in
    A. slipform paving   B. thin walls
    C. high early strength concrete D. tremic concrete

21. Given the dry weight of sand, the weight of damp sand can be estimated by assuming the weight of the dry sand is increased by _____ percent.
    A. 5   B. 10   C. 15   D. 20

3 (#2)

22. The chemical used as a set accelerator is calcium
    A. sulfate   B. carbonate   C. chloride   D. sulfide

    22._____

23. The specifications for mixing concrete have a maximum allowable mixing time to prevent overmixing. A DISADVANTAGE of overmixing is that
    A. the concrete will set prematurely
    B. it may increase the amount of fine aggregate
    C. segregation in the concrete may result
    D. there will be an excess of entrained air

    23._____

24. The equation of a straight line through the point (4,2) and perpendicular to the line x+2y+4=0 is
    A. y+6=0   B. 2y–x–6=0   C. y+2x-8=0   D. y-2x+6=0

    24._____

25. The equation of a straight line whose y intercept is 6 and whose x intercept is 4 is _____ = 0.
    A. y+2x-6   B. y-2x-6   C. 4x+67-24   D. 3x+2y-12

    25._____

KEY (CORRECT ANSWERS)

1. B
2. B
3. B
4. C
5. B

6. B
7. C
8. C
9. A
10. A

11. B
12. D
13. D
14. A
15. C

16. B
17. D
18. A
19. C
20. D

21. B
22. C
23. B
24. D
25. D

TEST 3

DIRECTIONS: Each question or incomplete statement is followed by several suggested answers or completions. Select the one that BEST answers the question or completes the statement. *PRINT THE LETTER OF THE CORRECT ANSWER IN THE SPACE AT THE RIGHT.*

1. If vector a = a_1i + b_1j + c_1k and vector b = b_1i + b_2i + b_3k, the dot product a.b is equal to
   A. $a_1b_1 + a_2b_2 + a_3b_3$
   B. $a_1a_2a_3 + b_1b_2b_3$
   C. $\begin{bmatrix} i & j & k \\ a_1 & a_2 & a_3 \\ b_1 & b_2 & b_3 \end{bmatrix}$
   D. $a_1b_2 + a_2b_3 + a_3b_1$

   1.____

2. If vector a = 3i + 4j and vector b = i + 2j, the projection of vector a on vector b is
   A. $\frac{11}{5}$
   B. $\frac{11\sqrt{5}}{5}$
   C. 11
   D. $11\sqrt{5}$

   2.____

3. Of the following vector operations, the one that is NOT commutative is
   A. a + b
   B. a − b
   C. a.b
   D. a×b

   3.____

4. The equation of a line is ax + by + c = 0. The length of a perpendicular from the origin to the line is
   A. $P = \left|\frac{c}{\sqrt{a^2+b^2}}\right|$
   B. $\left|\frac{c}{\sqrt{a^2+b^2+c^2}}\right|$
   C. $\left|\frac{c}{\sqrt{a+b}}\right|$
   D. $\frac{c}{\sqrt{a+b+c}}$

   4.____

5. The volume of a parallelepiped whose sides are vectors a, b, and c is
   A. a·b×c
   B. a·b·c
   C. a×b×c
   D. $\sqrt{a \times b \times c}$

   5.____

6. Matrix A = $\begin{bmatrix} 3 & 5 \\ 7 & -1 \end{bmatrix}$, Matrix B = $\begin{bmatrix} 4 & -3 \\ 6 & 1 \end{bmatrix}$. AB is equal to
   A. $\begin{bmatrix} -3 & 11 \\ 43 & 1 \end{bmatrix}$
   B. $\begin{bmatrix} 42 & -4 \\ 22 & -22 \end{bmatrix}$
   C. $\begin{bmatrix} -3 & 4 \\ 35 & -18 \end{bmatrix}$
   D. $\begin{bmatrix} -3 & -15 \\ 40 & -1 \end{bmatrix}$

   6.____

7. The volume of the solid shown at the right, in cubic feet, is
   A. 54
   B. 55
   C. 56
   D. 57

   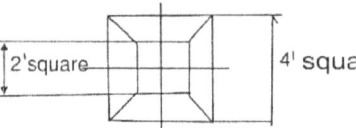
   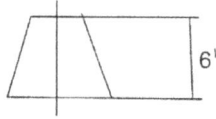

   7.____

8. The center of gravity, $\bar{x}$, of the shaded area shown at the right is
   A. 7.0
   B. 7.5
   C. 8.0
   D. 8.5

   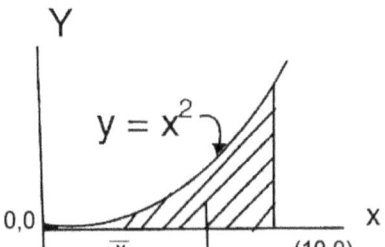

   8.____

2 (#3)

9. The determinant shown at the right is equal to 9._____

   A. -79   B. -88   C. -97   D. -106

10. The one of the following that is NOT an elementary matrix is 10._____

   A. $\begin{vmatrix} 1 & 0 & 2 \\ 0 & 1 & 0 \\ 0 & 0 & 1 \end{vmatrix}$ B. $\begin{vmatrix} 1 & 0 & 1 \\ 0 & 1 & 0 \\ 1 & 0 & 1 \end{vmatrix}$ C. $\begin{vmatrix} 1 & 0 & 0 \\ 0 & 2 & 0 \\ 0 & 0 & 1 \end{vmatrix}$ D. $\begin{vmatrix} 0 & 0 & 1 \\ 0 & 1 & 0 \\ 1 & 0 & 0 \end{vmatrix}$

11. The one of the following that is NOT a linear transformation is 11._____

   A. $L(2\alpha)$
   B. $L\left(\begin{bmatrix} a_1 \\ a_2 \end{bmatrix}\right) = \begin{bmatrix} ra_1 \\ ra_2 \end{bmatrix}$
   C. $L(at^2\_bt+c) = 2at+b$
   D. $L(2\alpha+1)$

12. The inverse of matrix $\begin{bmatrix} 1 & 2 \\ 3 & 4 \end{bmatrix}$ is 12._____

   A. $\begin{bmatrix} 2 & 1 \\ 3 & \frac{1}{2} \end{bmatrix}$ B. $\begin{bmatrix} 1 & \frac{3}{2} \\ 2 & -\frac{1}{2} \end{bmatrix}$ C. $\begin{bmatrix} -2 & 1 \\ \frac{3}{2} & -\frac{1}{2} \end{bmatrix}$ D. $\begin{bmatrix} \frac{3}{2} & \frac{1}{2} \\ 01 & 2 \end{bmatrix}$

13. $ax + by = c$ 13._____
    $dx + ey = 1$
    The value of x according to the Cramer Rule is x =

   A. $\dfrac{\begin{vmatrix} a & c \\ d & f \end{vmatrix}}{\begin{vmatrix} a & b \\ d & e \end{vmatrix}}$ B. $\dfrac{\begin{vmatrix} a & b \\ d & e \end{vmatrix}}{\begin{vmatrix} a & c \\ d & f \end{vmatrix}}$ C. $\dfrac{\begin{vmatrix} a & d \\ b & e \end{vmatrix}}{\begin{vmatrix} c & b \\ f & e \end{vmatrix}}$ D. $\dfrac{\begin{vmatrix} c & b \\ f & e \end{vmatrix}}{\begin{vmatrix} a & b \\ d & e \end{vmatrix}}$

14. The vector resulting from $(2i-3j+k)\times(i+j+k)$ is 14._____
    A. $-4i-j+5k$ B. $-3i+j-2k$ C. $4i-j+2k$ D. $3i+j-5k$

15. $(i\times j)\cdot k$ is equal to 15._____
    A. 1   B. 0   C. -1   D. $\sqrt{2}$

Questions 16-20.

DIRECTIONS: Questions 16 through 20, inclusive, refer to the stresses and forces in a rectangular beam.

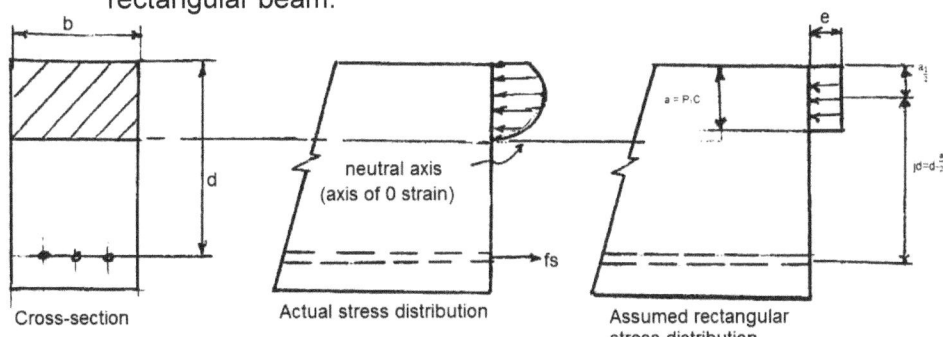

16. The strain in the concrete at failure is 16._____
    A. .001   B. .002   C. .003   D. .004

3 (#3)

17. The stress in the concrete denoted by letter e is
    A. .85f'c   B. .875f'c   C. .90f'c   D. .925 f'c

    17._____

18. The MINIMUM ratio of steel to concrete is equal to
    A. $\frac{200}{fy}$ B. $\frac{250}{fy}$ C. $\frac{300}{fy}$ D. $\frac{350}{fy}$

    18._____

19. The maximum ratio of steel to concrete in the above section is kp_b, where k is a constant and p_b is reinforcement ratio in the balanced strain condition. The value of k is
    A. 0.70   B. 0.75   C. 0.80   D. 0.85

    19._____

20. The reason for requiring a maximum ratio of steel to concrete is
    A. the design is uneconomical if Ag is too large
    B. there may not be enough space for the steel
    C. if the beam is overloaded, the concrete may collapse
    D. the steel may reach its yield point before the concrete

    20._____

21. The manufacturers of reinforcing bars now use the Soft Metric Bar Size designation. The #10 size bar in the Soft Metric Bar Size designation corresponds to, in the Inch-Pound Bar Size designation, to the _____ bar.
    A. #3   B. #4   C. #5   D. #6

    21._____

22. The tension development length for epoxy-coated bars, compared to non-coated bars, is
    A. greater than the non-epoxy-coated bar of the same size
    B. the same as the non-epoxy-coated bar of the same size
    C. smaller than the non-epoxy-coated bar of the same size
    D. greater or less than the non-epoxy-coated bar, depending on whether lightweight concrete or regular concrete is used

    22._____

23. The size sieve that separates fine aggregate for concrete from coarse aggregate is number
    A. 1½   B. 3   C. 4   D. 6

    23._____

24. The specific gravity of portland cement is assumed to be
    A. 3.05   B. 3.10   C. 3.15   D. 3.20

    24._____

25. A hydraulic cement included in portland cement is
    A. vermiculite   B. pozzolan   C. gypsum   D. cryolite

    25._____

KEY (CORRECT ANSWERS)

1.	A	11.	D
2.	B	12.	C
3.	D	13.	D
4.	A	14.	A
5.	A	15.	A
6.	B	16.	C
7.	C	17.	A
8.	B	18.	A
9.	C	19.	B
10.	B	20.	C

21. A
22. A
23. C
24. C
25. B

TEST 4

DIRECTIONS: Each question or incomplete statement is followed by several suggested answers or completions. Select the one that BEST answers the question or completes the statement. *PRINT THE LETTER OF THE CORRECT ANSWER IN THE SPACE AT THE RIGHT.*

1. A drawback in the use of an air-entraining agent in a concrete mix is that it
   A. reduces the slump in the concrete
   B. reduces the compressive strength of the concrete
   C. makes the concrete less water-resistant
   D. reduces the adhesion between the cement paste and the aggregates

   1.____

2. The *conjugate* beam for the beam shown at the right is

   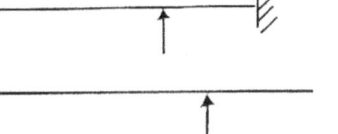

   A.    B.

   C. (similar to A)   D. (two upward arrows on a beam)

   2.____

3.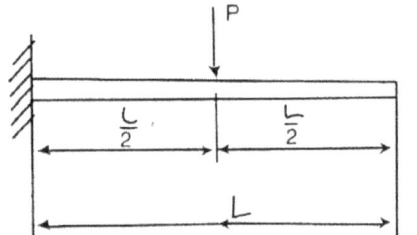

   The deflection at E on the cantilever beam shown above at point E is
   A. $\dfrac{5PL^3}{36EI}$ B. $\dfrac{5PL^3}{48EI}$ C. $\dfrac{5PL^3}{54EI}$ D. $\dfrac{7PL^3}{60EI}$

   3.____

4.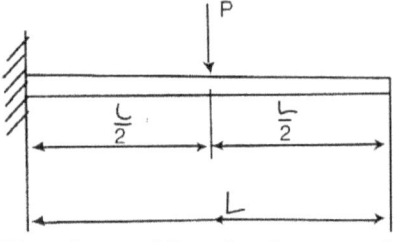

   The slope of the simply supported beam at E is
   A. $\dfrac{5PL^2}{128EI}$ B. $\dfrac{3PL^2}{80EI}$ C. $\dfrac{5PL^2}{96EI}$ D. $\dfrac{5PL^2}{72EI}$

   4.____

Questions 5-7.

DIRECTIONS: Questions 5 through 7, inclusive, refer to the following diagram.

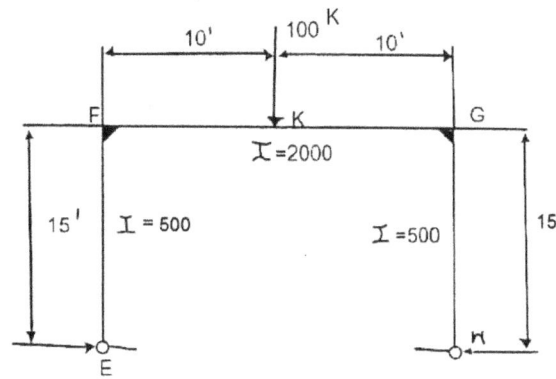

5. The moment at k, in foot kips, is
   A. 350 B. 400 C. 450 D. 500

6. The horizontal force at E, in kips, is
   A. 3.3 B. 6.7 C. 10 D. 13.3

7. The shear on beam FG at F, in kips, is
   A. 35 B. 40 C. 45 D. 50

8. The fixed end moment at E due to a load P is
   A. $\frac{Pab}{L^2}$
   B. $\frac{Pa^2b^2}{L^2}$
   C. $\frac{Pba^2}{L^2}$
   D. $\frac{Pab^2}{L^2}$

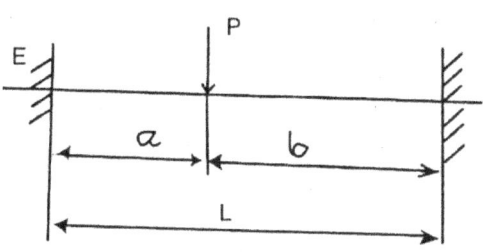

5.____

6.____

7.____

8.____

Questions 9-11.

DIRECTIONS: Questions 9 through 11, inclusive, refer to the following beam.

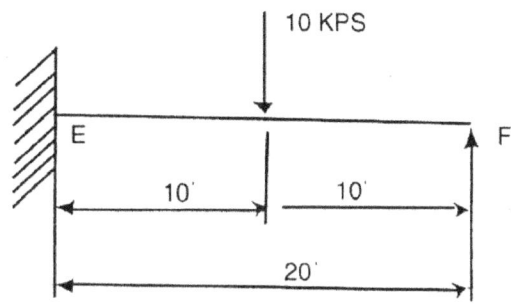

9. The end moment at E, in foot kips, is
   A. 35.0   B. 37.5   C. 40.0   D. 42.5

   9.____

10. The reaction at F, in kips, is
    A. 2.57   B. 2.87   C. 3.13   D. 3.39

    10.____

11. The conjugate beam would appear as pictured in diagram
    A. 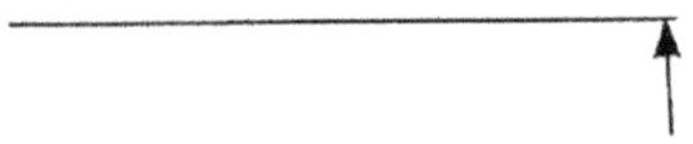
    B. 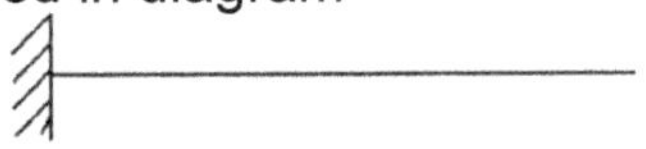
    C. 
    D.

    11.____

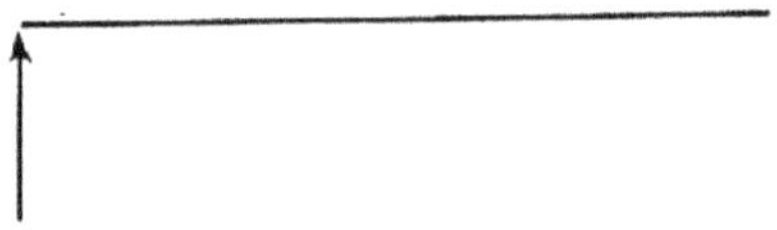

12. The maximum deflection on the beam shown at the right is
    A. $\dfrac{PL^3}{24EI}$
    B. $\dfrac{PL^3}{36EI}$
    C. $\dfrac{PL^3}{48EI}$
    D. $\dfrac{PL^3}{60EI}$

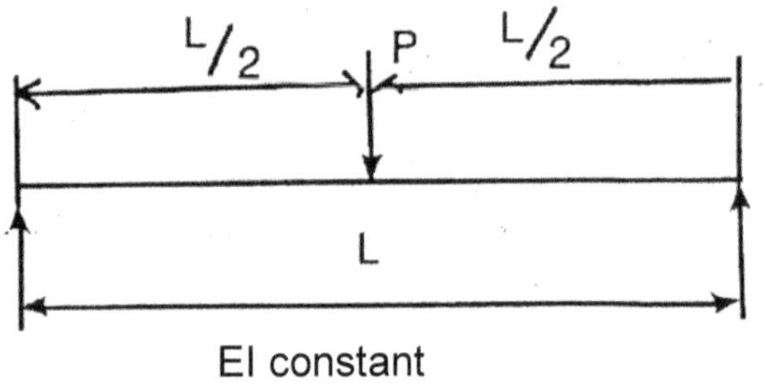

    EI constant

    12.____

13. The main reason for placing a concrete cradle under a large precast concrete sewer is to
    A. minimize settlement of the sewer
    B. prevent lateral displacement of the sewe
    C. minimize infiltration into the sewer
    D. strengthen the sewer against excessive vertical loads

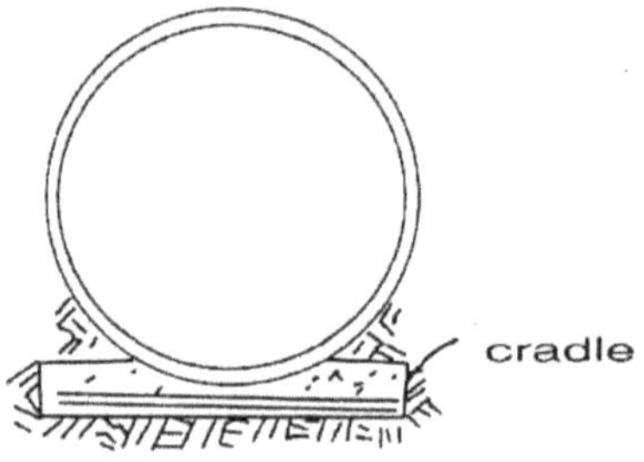

    13.____

14. The time of concentration would MOST likely be used in the design of _____ sewers.
    A. overflow   B. sanitary
    C. intercepting   D. storm

    14.____

15. Diversion chambers would MOST likely be found on _____ sewers.
    A. sanitary   B. intercepting
    C. storm   D. combined

    15.____

16. With the water depth at 2'0", neglecting friction, the minimum weight per foot W of the rectangular flap gate needed to prevent the water pushing the gate open is _____ pounds.
    A. 1210
    B. 1250
    C. 1290
    D. 1330

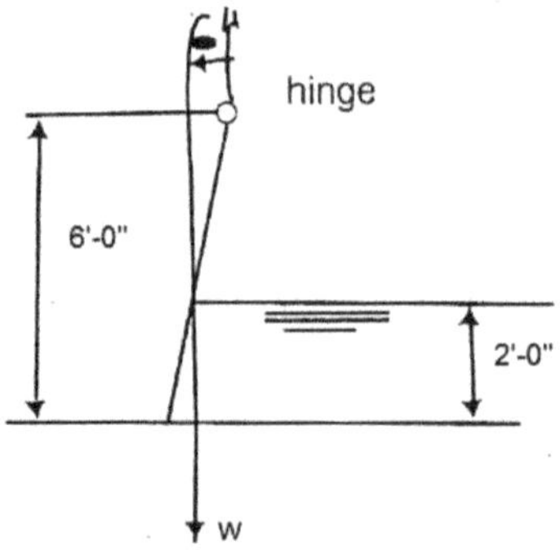

    16.____

17. For flow of water in circular pipes, the Reynolds number at which laminar flow changes to turbulent flow is
    A. 1500 B. 2000 C. 2500 D. 3000

18. The velocity distribution for laminar flow in a circular pipe is
    A. parabolic B. straight line
    C. circular D. elliptic

19. The center of gravity of the force P acting on the 4'0" x 4'0" gate is a distance y below the surface of _____ feet.
    A. 6.11
    B. 6.22
    C. 6.33
    D 6.44

20. The hydraulic radius with water flowing at a depth of 4 feet is
    A. 2.53 B. 2.63 C. 2.73 D. 2.83

21. One of the drawbacks of wood as a structural material is that it is anisotropic. This means that it
    A. is subject to decay
    B. has unequal physical properties along different axes
    C. has different moduli of elasticity depending upon the species of the lumber
    D. deteriorates with time

22. Lignin in wood
    A. is toxic to insects and termites
    B. impart color to the heartwood
    C. acts as an adhesive that glues the components of wood together
    D. is in the form of long-chain molecules in large groups that make up thread-like structures

23. A tropical wood that is used for piles is
    A. greenheart
    B. acacia
    C. lignum vitae
    D. baobab

24. Softwoods are trees that
    A. shed their leaves
    B. are typically evergreen
    C. are primarily used to make furniture
    D. have a higher modulus of elasticity than hardwoods

25. The moisture content of kiln-dried lumber when exposed to normal atmospheric conditions is _____% by weight.
    A. 5   B. 8   C. 11   D. 14

KEY (CORRECT ANSWERS)

1.	B	11.	A
2.	C	12.	C
3.	B	13.	A
4.	A	14.	D
5.	C	15.	B
6.	A	16.	D
7.	D	17.	B
8.	D	18.	A
9.	B	19.	B
10.	C	20.	B

21. B
22. C
23. A
24. B
25. C

EXAMINATION SECTION
TEST 1

DIRECTIONS: Each question or incomplete statement is followed by several suggested answers or completions. Select the one that BEST answers the question or completes the statement. *PRINT THE LETTER OF THE CORRECT ANSWER IN THE SPACE AT THE RIGHT.*

1. Which of the following types of estimates is considered BEST for estimating the total cost of a job?

    A. Unit cost estimate
    B. Lump-sum amount
    C. Cost-per-square-foot estimate
    D. Quantity survey

2. The scale of a typical set of architectural drawings uses _____ to represent 1 foot.

    A. 1/8"   B. 1/4"   C. 1/2"   D. 1"

3. A *square* in construction terms is an area of roofing that is _____ square feet.

    A. 40   B. 75   C. 100   D. 120

4. A _____ is represented by the mechanical symbol

    A. liquid pump
    B. water closet, flush valve
    C. compressor
    D. duct volume damper

5. Typically, a mud sill is bolted to a concrete foundation at intervals of _____ inches.

    A. 12-18   B. 18-36   C. 36-48   D. 48-60

6. For how many hours should an *A label* fire door be able to withstand continuous fire exposure?

    A. 3/4   B. 1   C. 1 1/2   D. 3

7. The current-carrying capacity of an electric device is USUALLY expressed in terms of

    A. voltage   B. amperage   C. gauge   D. resistance

8. Construction drawings show *quantities* via each of the following EXCEPT

    A. plans   B. sections
    C. specifications   D. details

9. What type of window consists of two or more sashes, one or more of which are moved horizontally?

    A. Transom   B. Sliding
    C. Casement   D. Double-hung

81

10. If boards are to be used for floor sheathing, the amount for cut-off ends and waste should be figured as _____% more than the floor space area to be sheathed.   10.____

    A. 5   B. 10   C. 20   D. 30

11. Grade B sheet glass can be used for glazing up to _____ square feet of area.   11.____

    A. 10   B. 16   C. 24   D. 30

12. What is generally considered to be the MAXIMUM roof pitch allowable for the use of roll roofing?   12.____
    _____ in 12.

    A. 2   B. 4   C. 6   D. 8

13. What is represented by the architectural symbol shown at the right?    13.____

    A. Stone concrete   B. Cinder concrete
    C. Gravel   D. Plaster

14. For estimating purposes, construction sound control methods are divided into each of the following major types EXCEPT   14.____

    A. construction with spaced studs and/or layered wall board
    B. absorbing material applied over wall or ceiling surfaces
    C. suspended ceilings
    D. sound-dampening floor covering

15. What is used to cover the ends of rafters in a cornice construction?   15.____

    A. Fascia   B. Hips
    C. Shears   D. Butt joints

16. Which of the following steps in a grading-quantity estimation would be performed FIRST?   16.____

    A. Determine approximate finish grade
    B. Calculate difference between cut and fill
    C. Estimate elevation of grid corners from contours
    D. Average the elevation of each grid square

17. What amount of masonry should a bricklayer and tender be able to install in an average work day?   17.____

    A. 50 square feet   B. 100 square feet
    C. 50 cubic feet   D. 100 linear feet

18. The time required for the placement labor and staking of slab-on-grade foundation forms should be calculated at APPROXIMATELY _____ hour(s) for 100 linear feet.   18.____

    A. 1/2   B. 1   C. 2 1/2   D. 3 1/2

19. What is represented by the mechanical symbol shown at the right? 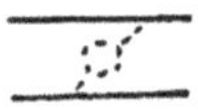   19.____

    A. Wall air outlet   B. Clean out
    C. Duct volume damper   D. Blower

20. What is the term for a steel pipe filled with concrete and used as a beam support? 20.____

   A. Bearing column B. Platform frame
   C. Lally column D. Soffit

21. Which of the following types of wood windows would be MOST expensive to install? 21.____

   A. Awning B. Casement
   C. Double-hung D. Horizontal sliding

22. A workman is installing 3 1/2-inch-thick batts of R-11 fiberglass insulation. 22.____
   About how many square feet will the workman be able to install in a typical work day?

   A. 300-500   B. 650-1000   C. 1200-1500   D. 1750-2000

23. What is represented by the architectural symbol shown at the right?  23.____

   A. Cast iron B. Aluminum
   C. Steel D. Brick

24. Most rafters are spaced _____ inches apart. 24.____

   A. 18   B. 24   C. 36   D. 48

25. What is the dividing strip within a window assembly that separates the various panes of glass? 25.____

   A. Muntin   B. Sash   C. Bunting   D. Mullion

KEY (CORRECT ANSWERS)

1. D   11. B
2. B   12. B
3. C   13. B
4. A   14. D
5. D   15. A

6. D   16. C
7. B   17. B
8. C   18. D
9. B   19. C
10. C   20. C

21. C
22. C
23. C
24. B
25. A

TEST 2

DIRECTIONS: Each question or incomplete statement is followed by several suggested answers or completions. Select the one that BEST answers the question or completes the statement. *PRINT THE LETTER OF THE CORRECT ANSWER IN THE SPACE AT THE RIGHT.*

1. What type of brick masonry unit is represented by the drawing shown at the right?
    A. Norman
    B. Economy
    C. King Norman
    D. Double

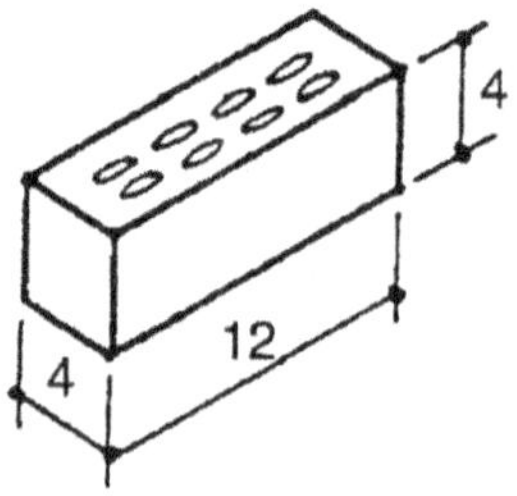

    1.____

2. The typical thickness of asphalt paving, applied over a gravel base course, is

    A. 1/2-2"   B. 1-3"   C. 2-5"   D. 3-7"

    2.____

3. Which of the following waterproofing materials is LEAST expensive?

    A. Two-ply polyethylene (.002")
    B. Sprayed-on bituminous coating
    C. Two-ply felt membrane
    D. Elastomeric waterproofing (1/32")

    3.____

4. Each of the following structures must always be included in an estimate if a *hip* roof is shown on drawings EXCEPT

    A. box cornice
    B. collar beam
    C. fascia
    D. solid sheathing

    4.____

5. What is represented by the electrical symbol shown at the right?

    A. Special purpose outlet
    B. Transformer
    C. Paging system
    D. Telephone

    5.____

6. The edge of a roof at the end of a building is called a

    A. sill   B. cornice   C. frieze   D. rake

    6.____

7. According to established finish-designation standards, which of the following finish materials would be ranked at the HIGHEST grade?

    A. White bronze
    B. Bright bronze
    C. Nickel-plated
    D. Cadmium-plated

    7.____

8. What is represented by the electrical symbol shown at the right?

    A. Duplex receptacle
    B. Call system
    C. Wall bracket light fixture
    D. Ceiling light fixture

    8.____

9. How many board-feet of rafters should two carpenters be able to install in a typical work day? 9.____

   A. 250 B. 500 C. 800 D. 1200

10. The valve at the LOWEST point of a water system is the 10.____

    A. drain cock B. globe valve
    C. check valve D. ball cock

11. When purchasing siding, what percentage of the material should typically be calculated as waste? 11.____

    A. 10% B. 15% C. 25% D. 35%

12. Which of the following is considered a *variable* overhead cost? 12.____

    A. Business permit B. Storage space
    C. Job permit D. Office utilities

13. What is the MOST commonly used paint base for use in kitchens and baths? 13.____

    A. Oil latex B. Oleoresin
    C. Urethane D. Alkyd enamel

14. Approximately how many linear feet of caulking material would be required for each door/window opening? 14.____

    A. 5-10 B. 12-15 C. 18-20 D. 22-28

15. What type of window is hinged at the side and opens outward from the opposite edge? 15.____

    A. Awning B. Casement C. Storm D. Sliding

16. Approximately how many square feet of particle board floor underlayment can be installed by a crew in a normal work day? 16.____

    A. 250 B. 750 C. 1200 D. 1500

17. What is represented by the architectural symbol shown at the right? 17.____

    A. Earth B. Sand C. Plaster D. Fire brick

18. Approximately how many linear feet of drywall tape will be required for 1000 square feet of area? 18.____

    A. 250 B. 400 C. 750 D. 1000

19. Which type of paving material can typically be applied MOST quickly? 19.____

    A. Asphalt B. Concrete, no curbs
    C. Random flagstone D. Concrete sidewalk

20. Approximately how many square feet of door and window surfaces should a painter be able to cover in one hour? 20.____

    A. 50 B. 75 C. 125 D. 175

21. What is the term for the thin coat of plaster applied to masonry or concrete walls to obtain a watertight or smooth surface?   21.____

    A. Plate   B. Laminate   C. Parging   D. Cripple

22. For estimating the labor cost of the installation of countertops and sink splashes, the typical tile labor time should be multiplied by   22.____

    A. 1/2   B. 2   C. 3   D. 4

23. In most retail stores, the markup for overhead profit is _____% over the wholesale cost of the material.   23.____

    A. 7-10   B. 12-25   C. 33-50   D. 40-60

24. When making wall covering estimates, the general practice is to add _____% to the cost of materials to account for waste and pattern matching.   24.____

    A. 10   B. 20   C. 35   D. 45

25. The underside of a cornice, beam, or any other material is known as a   25.____

    A. screed   B. section   C. truss   D. soffit

KEY (CORRECT ANSWERS)

1.	C	11.	A
2.	B	12.	C
3.	A	13.	D
4.	B	14.	C
5.	B	15.	B
6.	D	16.	D
7.	A	17.	A
8.	D	18.	B
9.	C	19.	A
10.	A	20.	C

21. C
22. C
23. C
24. B
25. D

TEST 3

DIRECTIONS: Each question or incomplete statement is followed by several suggested answers or completions. Select the one that BEST answers the question or completes the statement. *PRINT THE LETTER OF THE CORRECT ANSWER IN THE SPACE AT THE RIGHT.*

1. Approximately how many square feet of 4 1/4" x 4 1/4" glazed wall tile, applied with the adhesive-set method, can be applied in an average work day?

    A. 60   B. 130   C. 175   D. 220

    1.____

2. Which of the following would NOT be a typical R-value for fiberglass roll insulation material?

    A. R-8   B. R-11   C. R-23   D. R-30

    2.____

3. What is represented by the electrical symbol shown at the right?

    A. Signal push button
    B. Fluorescent light fixture
    C. Radio outlet
    D. Street light and bracket

    3.____

4. Generally, finishing hardware costs will be a MAXIMUM of _____% of the total job cost.

    A. .5   B. 1   C. 3   D. 7

    4.____

5. Built-up roofs are MOST often made from

    A. saturated felt
    B. tarpaper shingles
    C. wood shake
    D. tile

    5.____

6. What is represented by the architectural symbol shown at the right?

    A. Cut stone
    B. Concrete block
    C. Rubble stone
    D. Brick

    6.____

7. Most tubs, toilets, sinks, and lavatories require an average of _____ hours labor for the installation of rough plumbing.

    A. 3   B. 5   C. 7   D. 9

    7.____

8. What is the term for the inclined members of a stair that support the other members?

    A. Stringers   B. Slopes   C. Slumps   D. Risers

    8.____

9. Approximately how many square yards of diamond metal lath wall support can be installed in a typical work day?

    A. 30-40   B. 50-60   C. 75-85   D. 85-100

    9.____

10. What type of concrete masonry unit is represented by the drawing shown at the right?
    A. Double corner
    B. Soffit floor
    C. Corner
    D. Half cut header

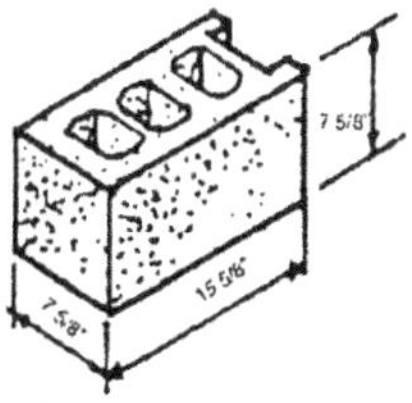

    10.____

11. Which of the following diameters would be MOST typical for a caisson hole?

    A. 12-24" B. 30-36" C. 40-48" D. 60-72"

12. One bundle of six gypsum lath will cover an area of _____ square feet of wall space.

    A. 18 B. 32 C. 48 D. 64

13. The estimate for cost of forms typically relies on

    A. surface contact feet
    B. cubic feet of foundation material
    C. material used as studs
    D. linear feet of forms

14. What is represented by the architectural symbol shown at the right?

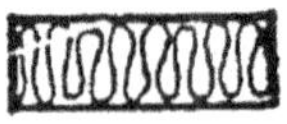

    A. Batted insulation   B. Vertical siding
    C. Concrete block   D. Ceramic tile

15. Approximately how many square feet of finish plywood siding can be installed by two carpenters in a typical work day?

    A. 200 B. 650 C. 850 D. 1200

16. After construction has begun, various fabricated items may require drawings that will indicate the exact size, shape, and material that the fabrication will have. These drawings are called

    A. detail drawings   B. shop drawings
    C. diagrams   D. specifications

17. How many bundles of roofing shakes, installed at 10" exposure, would be required to cover one square of roof area?

    A. 1 B. 3 C. 5 D. 7

18. What type of labor will normally be calculated for waterproofing work?

    A. Carpentry   B. Roofing
    C. Common labor   D. Tile

19. Which of the following is NOT generally classified as *rough* plumbing?

    A. Hot water line   B. Tub fixture
    C. Vent stack   D. Gas piping

20. Approximately how many square feet of 20-year bonded flat roofing can be installed by a crew in an average work day?

    A. 400-600   B. 750-1000
    C. 1200-1600   D. 1800-2000

21. Approximately how many hours of labor will be required for the machine sanding of 1000 square feet of unfinished wood strip flooring?

    A. 1/2 B. 1 C. 3 D. 4 1/2

22. What is represented by the mechanical symbol ⋈ shown at the right? 22.____

   A. Diaphragm valve B. Lock and shield valve
   C. Gate valve D. Check valve

23. Approximately how many linear feet of mud sill should a 2-person crew be able to install in a typical work day? 23.____

   A. 50-100 B. 150-250 C. 250-300 D. 350-400

24. When calculating the area of a gabled roof, the estimator should remember to multiply the initial figure by 24.____

   A. 1/4 B. 1/2 C. 2 D. 4

25. The calculation of the square-foot area of a building includes the area of the 25.____

   A. internal face B. basement
   C. attic D. external face

KEY (CORRECT ANSWERS)

1. C
2. A
3. B
4. C
5. A

6. B
7. B
8. A
9. B
10. C

11. B
12. B
13. A
14. A
15. B

16. B
17. C
18. B
19. B
20. D

21. B
22. C
23. C
24. C
25. D

EXAMINATION SECTION
TEST 1

DIRECTIONS: Each question or incomplete statement is followed by several suggested answers or completions. Select the one that BEST answers the question or completes the statement. *PRINT THE LETTER OF THE CORRECT ANSWER IN THE SPACE AT THE RIGHT.*

1. A percentage of the payment for a contract is held back until the job is completed for one year.
   The MAIN reason for this practice is to insure that the

   A. city doesn't overpay the contractor for the job
   B. contractor will return to correct defective work after the job is completed
   C. contractor will not make unwarranted claims against the city
   D. contractor will pay all his subcontractors

   1.____

2. There are four separate major contracts on a certain building construction project.
   The MAJOR disadvantage of this practice, as compared to the practice of having a single contract, is

   A. the difficulty in coordinating the work
   B. the low level of productivity of the tradesman
   C. cost of the material going into the building is greater
   D. the difficulty in finding competent bidders on the contracts

   2.____

3. Of the following, the PREFERRED way to authorize a contractor to perform work other than required by the contract is by a

   A. T & M order   B. unit price order
   C. lump sum modification D. change order

   3.____

4. A contract requires that the prime contractor do a certain minimum percentage of the work with his own forces.
   Of the following, the BEST reason for this requirement is to

   A. insure good work
   B. discourage bidders who may not have the ability to do the job
   C. encourage more people to bid the job, thus lowering the bid price
   D. freeze out incompetent subcontractors

   4.____

5. In computing an extra based on the actual cost of work done, the THREE MAJOR items that go into the cost are

   A. taxes, labor, and material
   B. time, taxes, and material
   C. labor, material, and equipment
   D. taxes, labor, and equipment

   5.____

6. A contractor is to be penalized if he exceeds a certain completion date. There is a major strike lasting a month that shuts down all construction.
   Under these conditions, the completion date should be

   6.____

A. held unchanged
B. made two weeks later than the original date
C. made one month later than the original date
D. made six weeks later than the original completion date

7. The one of the following that refers to a Federal safety program in construction is   7.____

   A. OSHA   B. AISC   C. AIEE   D. UL

8. With regard to the placing of concrete, the contractor is GENERALLY   8.____

   A. limited to a specific method by the contract
   B. not permitted to rent equipment to place the concrete
   C. not permitted to pump the concrete into place
   D. permitted to choose his own method of placing the concrete

9. The MOST practical control the inspector or resident engineer has over the contractor when the inspector is not satisfied with the quality of the work is to   9.____

   A. discuss withholding payment on that part of the work that is unsatisfactory
   B. threaten to have the contractor thrown off the job
   C. request that the contractor fire the men responsible for the unsatisfactory work
   D. call the owner of the company and explain the situation to him

10. The MOST practical method of being sure that the architect will be satisfied with the appearance of the exterior brick work for a building is to   10.____

    A. build a sample wall section, for the architect's approval, with the brick that is delivered to the job site
    B. send the architect to the plant supplying the brick to insure that the color and tone of the brick is satisfactory
    C. have the architect's representative on the job while the brick work is being erected to be sure the finished product is satisfactory
    D. put a damage clause in the contract penalizing the contractor if the brick work is not satisfactory to the architect

11. Of the following, the MOST frequent problem that will arise during the construction of a building is   11.____

    A. inability to fit all the reinforcing steel in the space allotted to it
    B. interference in piping and ductwork
    C. inability to keep walls level
    D. settling of the foundation as the load comes on the building

12. To find the number of reinforcing bars that should be in a slab, the inspector SHOULD refer to the   12.____

    A. architect's plan
    B. reinforcing steel design drawings
    C. standard detail drawings
    D. reinforcing steel detail drawings

13. The specifications for a building state that a certain brick type shall be *Stark Brick type XX or equal.*
    The BEST reason for inserting the *or equal* clause is to

    A. permit other companies to compete in supplying the brick
    B. allow other companies to submit their product to determine which is best
    C. limit the suppliers only to those companies whose product is superior to that produced by Stark
    D. allow Stark Brick Company to set the standard for the industry

14. In the absence of a formal training program for inspectors, the BEST of the following ways to train a new man who is to do inspection work is to

    A. give him the literature on the subject so that he can learn what he has to know
    B. have him accompany an inspector as the inspector does his work so that he can learn by observing
    C. assign him the job and let him learn on his own
    D. tell him to go to a school at night that specializes in this field so that he will gain the necessary background

15. Of the following, the safety practice that is REQUIRED on the construction job site is

    A. safety shoes must be worn by all workers
    B. safety goggles must be worn by all workers
    C. safety helmets must be worn by all workers
    D. all workers must have a safety kit in their possession

16. Safety on the job is the concern of

    A. the individual workman only
    B. the contractor only
    C. all parties on the job
    D. the insuring company only

17. Frequently, payments due the contractor are delayed many months because of a backlog of work in the agency.
    This practice is considered

    A. *good* because the city saves money by delaying payment
    B. *poor* because the contractors will raise their bids in the future to compensate for the added cost
    C. *poor* because it becomes difficult to compute payments
    D. *good* because it forces the contractor to do good work in order to be sure that he will receive payment

18. Provisions are made in a contract for payment for certain items when delivered to the job before installation.
    The MAIN reason for this practice is to

    A. enable better inspection of the items
    B. prevent bottlenecks during construction
    C. give the contractor a quick profit on the items
    D. allow the contractor more time to shop for the items

19. The agency that approves payments to building contractors is the 19.____

   A. Corporation Counsel B. Comptroller's Office
   C. Board of Estimate   D. City Planning Commission

20. The bond that the contractor puts up to insure that he will start work is the 20.____

   A. Bid Bond   B. Payment Bond
   C. Performance Bond   D. Liability Insurance

21. Of the following, the BEST practice to follow in order to minimize claims of damage to adjacent buildings during the construction of a building is to 21.____

   A. take out special insurance against such claims
   B. make a detailed survey of the condition of the nearby buildings before construction begins
   C. make a payment to adjacent property owners in advance so that they waive claims of damage to their property
   D. have the buildings underpinned

22. The four MAJOR contracts on a building project are: 22.____

   A. General Construction, Electrical, Plumbing and Drainage, Heating, Ventilating and Air Conditioning
   B. Plumbing, Heating and Ventilating, Air Conditioning, and General Construction
   C. Foundations, Superstructure, Mechanical, and Electrical
   D. Air Conditioning, Electrical, Mechanical, and Structural

23. Oil tanks, when set in place inside a building, are frequently filled with water. 23.____
   The BEST reason for this practice is

   A. to prevent them from floating off their foundation if water fills the room
   B. to enable them to be lifted up more easily
   C. to prevent them from becoming rusted
   D. for emergency use in case of fire

24. The filing system used in the field for correspondence is required to be uniform for all jobs. 24.____
   The BEST reason for this requirement is that

   A. there is only one good way of setting up the filing system
   B. the standardized system is compact, thereby saving space
   C. other interested parties such as engineers from the main office will be able to use the files
   D. the contractor's forces will understand the filing system and will be able to extract necessary correspondence

25. Upon excavation to the subgrade of a footing to be placed on piles, the inspector finds that the soil is very poor. 25.____
   Of the following, the PROPER action for the inspector to take is to

   A. do nothing
   B. add 20% to the number of piles
   C. notify the engineer's office of this condition
   D. order the contractor to keep excavating until he hits better soil

26. The general contractor is required to submit a progress schedule before starting work. Of the following, the BEST reason for this requirement is to

    A. determine if the contractor intends to complete the job
    B. enable the inspector to determine whether the contractor is on schedule
    C. enable the inspector to estimate monthly payments
    D. check minority hiring

27. If a contractor is falling behind schedule, the FIRST thing to check if the inspector is looking for the cause of this condition is the

    A. number of men he has on the job
    B. efficiency of his crew
    C. availability of equipment needed to do the job
    D. availability of the latest drawings needed by the contractor

28. The critical path method is a method for

    A. finding the best material needed for a specific use
    B. determining the best arrangement of equipment
    C. determining the best time to replace a piece of machinery
    D. scheduling work

29. The contractor states to the inspector that a given structural detail is undersized and unsafe.
    Of the following, the BEST action for the inspector to take in this situation is to

    A. ignore the complaint since the contractor is not an engineer
    B. change the detail by issuing a change order
    C. notify your superiors of the contractor's statements
    D. allow the contractor to modify the detail since it is his responsibility

30. The contractor proposes to use an additive to the concrete to accelerate its set. He asks you, the inspector, for permission to use it.
    Of the following, the FIRST action to take in response to his request is to

    A. check if the use of the additive is permitted by the specifications
    B. tell him to put the request in writing
    C. ask your superior if the use of the additive is acceptable
    D. deny him permission since additives to concrete are not permitted

KEY (CORRECT ANSWERS)

1.	B	16.	C
2.	A	17.	B
3.	D	18.	B
4.	B	19.	B
5.	C	20.	A
6.	C	21.	B
7.	A	22.	A
8.	D	23.	A
9.	A	24.	C
10.	A	25.	A
11.	B	26.	B
12.	D	27.	A
13.	A	28.	D
14.	B	29.	C
15.	C	30.	A

EXAMINATION SECTION
TEST 1

DIRECTIONS: Each question or incomplete statement is followed by several suggested answers or completions. Select the one that BEST answers the question or completes the statement. *PRINT THE LETTER OF THE CORRECT ANSWER IN THE SPACE AT THE RIGHT.*

1. A *basic* method of operation that a *good* supervisor should follow is to

    A. check the work of subordinates constantly to make sure they are not making exceptions to the rules
    B. train subordinates so they can handle problems that come up regularly themselves and come to him only with special cases
    C. delegate to subordinates only those duties which he cannot do himself
    D. issue directions to subordinates only on special matters

    1.____

2. To do a *good* job of performance evaluation, it is BEST for a supervisor to

    A. compare the employee's performance to that of another employee doing similar work
    B. give greatest weight to instances of unusually good or unusually poor performance
    C. leave out any consideration of the employee's personal traits
    D. measure the employee's performance against standard performance requirements

    2.____

3. Of the following, the MOST important reason for a supervisor to have private face to face discussions with subordinates about their performance is to

    A. help employees improve their work
    B. give special praise to employees who perform well
    C. encourage the employees to compete for higher performance ratings
    D. discipline employees who perform poorly

    3.____

4. Of the following, the CHIEF purpose of a probationary period for a new employee is to allow time for

    A. finding out whether the selection processes are satisfactory
    B. the employee to make adjustments in his home circumstances made necessary by the job
    C. the employee to decide whether he wants a permanent appointment
    D. determining the fitness of the employee to continue in the job

    4.____

5. When a subordinate resigns his job, it is MOST important to conduct an exit interview in order to

    A. try to get the employee to remain on the job
    B. learn the true reasons for the employee's resignation
    C. see that the employee leaves with a good opinion of the agency
    D. ask the employee if he would consider a transfer

    5.____

6. Chronic lateness of employees is generally LEAST likely to be due to

    A. distance of job location from home   B. poor personnel administration
    C. unexpressed employee grievances   D. low morale

    6.____

7. Of the following, the LEAST effective stimulus for motivating employees toward inproved performance over a long-range period is

   A. their sense of achievement
   B. their feeling of recognition
   C. opportunity for their self-development
   D. an increase in salary

8. Suppose that NOT ONE of a group of employees has turned in an idea to the employees suggestion system during the past year.
   The *most probable* reason for this situation is that the

   A. money awards given for suggestions used are not high enough to make employees interested
   B. employees in this group are not able to develop any good ideas
   C. supervisor of these employees is not doing enough to encourage them to take part in the program
   D. methods and procedures of operation do not need improvement

9. A subordinate tells you that he is having trouble concentrating on his work due to a personal problem at home.
   Of the following, it would be BEST for you to

   A. refer him to a community service agency
   B. listen quietly to the story because he may just need a sympathetic ear
   C. tell him that you cannot help him because the problem is not job related
   D. ask him questions about the nature of the problem and tell him how you would handle it

10. For you as a supervisor to give each of your subordinates *exactly* the same type of supervision is

    A. *advisable*, because doing this insures fair and impartial treatment of each individual
    B. *not advisable*, because individuals like to think that they are receiving better treatment than others
    C. *advisable*, because once a supervisor learns how to deal with a subordinate who brings a problem to him, he can handle another subordinate with this problem in the same way
    D. *not advisable*, because each person is different and there is no one supervisory procedure for dealing with individuals that applies in every case

11. A senior employee under your supervision tells you that he is reluctant to speak to one of his subordinates about his poor work habits, because this worker is "strong-willed" and he does not want to antagonize him.
    For you to offer to speak to the subordinate about this matter yourself would be

    A. *advisable*, since you are in a position of greater authority
    B. *inadvisable*, since handling this problem is a basic supervisory responsibility of the senior employee
    C. *advisable*, since the senior employee must work more closely with the worker than you do
    D. *inadvisable*, since you should not risk antagonizing the employee yourself

12. Some of your subordinates have been coming to you with complaints you feel are unimportant. For you to hear their stories out is

    A. *poor practice,* you should spend your time on more important matters
    B. *good practice,* this will increase your popularity with your subordinates
    C. *poor practice,* subordinates should learn to come to you only with major grievances
    D. *good practice,* it may prevent minor complaints from developing into major grievances

13. Assume that an agency has an established procedure for handling employee grievances. An employee in this agency, comes to his immediate supervisor with a grievance. The supervisor investigates the matter and makes a decision.
    However, the employee is not satisfied with the decision made by the supervisor. The BEST action for the supervisor to take is to

    A. tell the employee he will review the matter further
    B. remind the employee that he is the supervisor and the employee must act in accordance with his decision
    C. explain to the employee how he can carry his complaint forward to the next step in the grievance procedure
    D. tell the employee he will consult with his own superiors on the matter

14. Subordinate employees and senior employees often must make quick decisions while in the field. The supervisor can BEST help subordinates meet such situations by

    A. training them in the appropriate action to take for every problem that may come up
    B. limiting the areas in which they are permitted to make decisions
    C. making certain they understand clearly the basic policies of the bureau and the department
    D. delegating authority to make such decisions to only a few subordinates on each level

15. Studies have shown that the CHIEF cause of failure to achieve success as a supervisor is

    A. an unwillingness to delegate authority to subordinates
    B. the establishment of high performance standards for subordinates
    C. the use of discipline that is too strict
    D. showing too much leniency to poor workers

16. When a supervisor delegates to a subordinate certain work that he normally does himself, it is MOST important that he give the subordinate

    A. responsibility for also setting the standards for the work to be done
    B. sufficient authority to be able to carry out the assignment
    C. written, step-by-step instructions for doing the work
    D. an explanation of one part of the task at a time

17. It is particularly important that disciplinary actions be equitable as between individuals. This statement *implies* that

    A. punishment applied in disciplinary actions should be lenient
    B. proposed disciplinary actions should be reviewed by higher authority
    C. subordinates should have an opportunity to present their stories before penalties are applied
    D. penalties for violations of the rules should be standardized and consistently applied

18. You discover that from time to time a number of false rumors circulate among your subordinates.
    Of the following, the BEST way for you to handle this situation is to

    A. ignore the rumors since rumors circulate in every office and can never be eliminated
    B. attempt to find those responsible for the rumors and reprimand them
    C. make sure that your employees are informed as soon as possible about all matters that affect them
    D. inform your superior about the rumors and let him deal with the matter

19. Supervisors who allow the "halo effect" to influence their evaluations of subordinates are *most likely* to

    A. give more lenient ratings to older employees who have longer service
    B. let one highly favorable or unfavorable trait unduly affect their judgment of an employee
    C. evaluate all employees on one trait before considering a second
    D. give high evaluations in order to avoid antagonizing their subordinates

20. For a supervisor to keep records of reprimands to subordinates about infractions of the rules is

    A. *good practice,* because these records are valuable to support disciplinary actions recommended or taken
    B. *poor practice,* because such records are evidence of the supervisor's inability to maintain discipline
    C. *good practice,* because such records indicate that the supervisor is doing a good job
    D. *poor practice,* because the best way to correct subordinates is to give them more training

21. When a new departmental policy has been established, it would be MOST advisable for you, as a supervisor, to

    A. distribute a memo which states the new policy and instruct your subordinates to read it
    B. explain specifically to your subordinates how the policy is going to affect them
    C. make sure your subordinates understand that you are not responsible for setting the policy
    D. tell your subordinates whether you agree or disagree with the policy

22. As a supervisor, you receive several complaints about the rude conduct of a subordinate. The FIRST action you should take is to

    A. request his transfer to another office
    B. prepare a charge sheet for disciplinary action
    C. assign a senior employee to work with him for a week
    D. interview the employee to determine possible reason, and warn that correction is necessary

23. A supervisor is *most likely* to get subordinates to work cooperatively toward accomplishing bureau goals if he

    A. creates an atmosphere that contributes to their feeling of security
    B. backs up subordinates even when they occasionally disobey regulations
    C. shows interest in subordinates by helping them solve their personal problems
    D. uses an authoritarian or "bossy" approach to supervision

24. A supervisor is holding a staff meeting with his senior employees to try to find an acceptable solution to a problem that has come up.
    Of the following, the CHIEF role of the supervisor at this meeting should be to

    A. see that every member of the group contributes at least one suggestions
    B. act as chairman of the meeting, but take no other active part to avoid influencing the senior employees
    C. keep the participants from wandering off into discussions of irrelevant matters
    D. make certain the participants hear his views on the matter at the beginning of the meeting

25. An employee shows you a certificate that he has just received for completing two years of study in conversational Spanish. As his supervisor, it would be BEST for you to

    A. put a note about this accomplishment in his personnel folder
    B. assign him to areas in which people of Spanish origin live
    C. congratulate him on this accomplishment, but tell him frankly that you doubt this is likely to have any direct bearing on his work
    D. encourage him to continue his studies and become thoroughly fluent in speaking the language

KEY (CORRECT ANSWERS)

1.	B	11.	B
2.	D	12.	D
3.	A	13.	C
4.	D	14.	C
5.	B	15.	A
6.	A	16.	B
7.	D	17.	D
8.	C	18.	C
9.	B	19.	B
10.	D	20.	A

21. B
22. D
23. A
24. C
25. A

TEST 2

DIRECTIONS: Each question or incomplete statement is followed by several suggested answers or completions. Select the one that BEST answers the question or completes the statement. *PRINT THE LETTER OF THE CORRECT ANSWER IN THE SPACE AT THE RIGHT.*

1. Of the following, the factor affecting employee morale which the immediate supervisor is LEAST able to control is 1.____

    A. handling of grievances
    B. fair and impartial treatment of subordinates
    C. general presonnel rules and regulations
    D. accident prevention

2. When one of your workers does outstanding work, you should 2.____

    A. explain to your other employees that you expect the same kind of work of them
    B. praise him for his work so that he will know it is appreciated
    C. say nothing, because other employees may think you are showing favoritism
    D. show him how his work can be improved still more so that he will not sit back

3. For you as a supervisor to consider a suggestion from a probationary worker for improving a procedure would be 3.____

    A. *poor practice,* because this employee is too new on the job to know much about it
    B. *good practice,* because you may be able to share credit for the suggestion
    C. *poor practice,* because it may hurt the morale of the older employees
    D. *good practice,* because the suggestion may be worthwhile

4. If you find you must criticize the work of one of your workers, it would be BEST for you to 4.____

    A. mention the good points in his work as well as the faults
    B. caution him that he will receive an unsatisfactory performance report unless his work improves
    C. compare his work to that of the other agents you supervise
    D. apologize for making the criticism

5. As a senior employee which one of the following matters would it be BEST for you to talk over with your supervisor before you take final action? 5.____

    A. One of the workers you supervise continues to disregard your instructions repeatedly in spite of repeated warnings
    B. One of your workers tells you he wants to discuss a personal problem
    C. A probationary employee tells you he does not understand a procedure
    D. One of your workers tells you he disagrees with the way you rate his work

6. If one of your subordinates asks you a question about a department rule and you do not know the answer, you should tell him that 6.____

    A. he should try to get the information himself
    B. you do not have the answer, but you will get it for him as soon as you can
    C. he should ask you the question again a week from now
    D. he should put the question in writing

7. If, as a supervisor, you realize that you have been unfair in criticizing one of your subordinates, the BEST action for you to take is to

   A. say nothing, but overlook some error made by this employee in the future
   B. be frank and tell the employee that you are sorry for the mistake you made
   C. let the employee know in some indirect way without admitting your mistake, that you realize he was not at fault
   D. say nothing, but be more careful about criticizing subordinates in the future

8. Of the following, the MOST important reason for a supervisor to write an accident report as soon as possible after an accident has happened is to

   A. make sure that important facts about the accident are not forgotten
   B. avoid delay in getting compensation for the injured person
   C. get adequate medical treatment for the injured person
   D. keep department accident statistics up to date

9. In any matter which may require disciplinary action, the FIRST responsibility of the supervisor is to

   A. decide what penalty should be applied for the offense
   B. refer the matter to a higher authority for complete investigation
   C. place the interests of the department above those of the employee
   D. investigate the matter fully to get all the facts

10. Suppose you find it necessary to criticize one of the subordinates you supervise. You should

    A. send an official letter to his home
    B. speak to him about the matter privately
    C. speak to him at a staff meeting
    D. ask another worker who is friendly with him to talk to him about the matter

11. Some of your subordinates have been coming to you with complaints you feel are unimportant. For you to hear their stories out is

    A. *poor practice,* you should spend your time on more important matters
    B. *good practice,* this will increase your popularity with your subordinates
    C. *poor practice,* subordinates should learn to come to you only with major grievances
    D. *good practice,* it may prevent minor complaints from developing into major grievances

12. Suppose that NOT ONE of a group of employees has turned in an idea to the employees' suggestion system during the past year. The *most probable* reason for this situation is that the

    A. supervisor of these employees is not doing enough to encourage them to take part in this program
    B. employees in this group are not able to develop any good ideas
    C. money awards given for suggestions used are not high enough to make employees interested
    D. methods and procedures of operation do not need improvement

13. For you as a supervisor to give each of your subordinates *exactly* the same type of supervision is

   A. *advisable,* because doing this insures fair and impartial treatment of each individual
   B. *not advisable,* because each person is different and there is no one supervisory procedure for dealing with individuals that applies in every case
   C. *advisable,* because once a supervisor learns how to deal with a subordinate who brings a problem to him, he can handle another subordinate with this problem in the same way
   D. *not advisable,* because individuals like to think that they are receiving better treatment than others

14. In evaluating personnel, a supervisor should keep in mind that the MOST important objective of performance evaluations is to

   A. encourage employees to compete for higher performance ratings
   B. give recognition to employees who perform well
   C. help employees improve their work
   D. discipline employees who perform poorly

15. A subordinate tells you that he is having trouble concentrating on his work due to a personal problem at home. Of the following, it would be BEST for you to

   A. refer him to a community service agency
   B. listen quietly to the story because he may just need a sympathetic ear
   C. tell him that you cannot help him because the problem is not job-related
   D. ask him some questions about the nature of the problem and tell him how you would handle it

16. To do a good job of performance evaluation, it is BEST for a supervisor to

   A. measure the employee's performance against standard performance requirements
   B. compare the employee's performance to that of another employee doing similar work
   C. leave out any consideration of the employee's personal traits
   D. give greatest weight to instances of unusually good or unusually poor performance

17. It is particularly important that disciplinary actions be equitable as between individuals. This statement *implies* that

   A. punishment applied in disciplinary actions should be lenient
   B. proposed disciplinary actions should be reviewed by higher authority
   C. subordinates should have an opportunity to present their stories before penalties are applied
   D. penalties for violations of the rules should be standardized and consistently applied

18. Assume that an agency has an established procedure for handling employee grievances. An employee in this agency comes to his immediate supervisor with a grievance. The supervisor investigates the matter and makes a decision. However, the employee is not satisfied with the decision made by the supervisor.
The BEST action for the supervisor to take is to

A. tell the employee he will review the matter further
B. remind the employee that he is the supervisor and the employee must act in accordance with his decision
C. explain to the employee how he can carry his complaint forward to the next step in the grievance procedure
D. tell the employee he will consult with his own superiors on the matter

19. Of the following, the CHIEF purpose of a probationary period for a new employee is to allow time for

    A. finding out whether the selection processes are satisfactory
    B. determining the fitness of the employee to continue in the job
    C. the employee to decide whether he wants a permanent appointment
    D. the employee to make adjustments in his home circumstances made necessary by the job

20. Of the following, the subject that would be MOST important to include in a "break-in" program for new employees is

    A. explanation of rules, regulations and policies of the agency
    B. Instruction in the agency's history and programs
    C. explanation of the importance of the new employees' own particular job
    D. explanation of the duties and responsibilities of the employee

21. Suppose a new employee under your supervision seems slow to learn and is making mistakes in performing his duties. Your FIRST action should be to

    A. pass this information on to the bureau director
    B. reprimand the worker so he will not repeat these mistakes
    C. find out whether this worker understands your instructions
    D. note these facts for future reference when writing up the monthly performance evaluation

22. In training new employees to do a certain job it would be LEAST desirable for you to

    A. demonstrate how the job is done, step by step
    B. encourage the workers to ask questions if they aren't clear about any point
    C. tell them about the various mistakes other agents have made in doing this job
    D. have the workers do the job, explaining to you what they are doing and why

23. One of the workers under your supervision is resentful when you ask her to remove her jangling bracelets before she starts her tour of duty.
    Of the following, the BEST explanation you can give her for the rule against wearing such jewelry while on duty is that

    A. the jewelry may create a safety hazard
    B. employees must give up certain personal liberties if they want to keep their jobs
    C. workers cannot perform their duties as efficiently if they wear distracting jewelry
    D. citizens may receive an unfavorable impression of the department

24. Of the following, the LEAST important reason for having a department handbook and a bureau standard operating procedure is to

    A. help in training new employees
    B. provide a source of reference for department and bureau rules and procedures
    C. prevent errors in work by providing clear guidelines
    D. make the supervisor's job easy

25. On inspecting your squad prior to their tour of duty, you note an employee improperly and unacceptably dressed.
    The FIRST action you should take is to

    A. call the employee aside and insist on immediate correction if possible
    B. notify the district commander right away
    C. have the employee submit a memorandum explaining the reason for the improper uniform
    D. permit the employee to proceed on duty but warn him not to let this happen again

KEY (CORRECT ANSWERS)

1. C	11. D
2. B	12. A
3. D	13. B
4. A	14. C
5. A	15. B
6. B	16. A
7. B	17. D
8. A	18. C
9. D	19. B
10. B	20. D

21. C
22. C
23. D
24. D
25. A

DOCUMENTS AND FORMS
PREPARING WRITTEN MATERIALS
EXAMINATION SECTION
TEST 1

DIRECTIONS: Each question or incomplete statement is followed by several suggested answers or completions. Select the one that BEST answers the question or completes the statement. *PRINT THE LETTER OF THE CORRECT ANSWER IN THE SPACE AT THE RIGHT.*

1. Of the following types of documents, it is MOST important to retain and file
   A. working drafts of reports that have been submitted in final form
   B. copies of letters of good will which conveyed a message that could not be handled by phone
   C. interoffice orders for materials which have been received and verified
   D. interoffice memoranda regarding the routine of standard forms

   1._____

2. The MAXIMUM number of 2¾" x 4¼" size forms which may be obtained from one ream of 17" x 22" paper is
   A. 4,000   B. 8,000   C. 12,000   D. 16,000

   2._____

3. On a general organization chart, staff positions NORMALLY should be pictured
   A. directly above the line positions to which they report
   B. to the sides of the main flow lines
   C. within the box of the highest level subordinate positions pictured
   D. directly below the line positions which report to them

   3._____

4. When an administrator is diagramming an office layout, of the following, his PRIMARY job generally should be to indicate the
   A. lighting intensities that will be required by each operator
   B. noise level that will be produced by the various equipment employed in the office
   C. direction of the work flow and the distance involved in each transfer
   D. durability of major pieces of office equipment currently in use or to be utilized

   4._____

5. One common guideline or rule-of-thumb ratio for evaluating the efficiency of files is the number of records requested divided by the number of records filed. Generally, if this ratio is very low, it would point MOST directly to the need for
   A. improving the indexing and coding systems
   B. improving the charge-out procedures
   C. exploring the need for transferring records from active storage to the archives
   D. exploring the need to encourage employees to keep more records in their private files

   5._____

2 (#1)

6. The GREATEST percentage of money spent on preparing and keeping the usual records in an office generally is expended for which one of the following?
   A. Renting space in which to place the record-keeping equipment
   B. Paying salaries of record-preparing and record-keeping personnel
   C. Depreciation of purchased record-preparation and record-keeping machines
   D. Paper and forms upon which to place the records

6._____

7. In a certain office, file folders are constantly being removed from the files for use by administrators. At the same time, new material is coming in to be filed in some of these folders.
Of the following, the BEST way to avoid delays in filing of the new material and to keep track of the removed folders is to
   A. keep a sheet listing all folders removed from the file, who has them, and a follow-update to check on their return; attach to this list new material received for filing
   B. put an "out" slip in the place of any file folder removed, telling what folder is missing, date removed, and who has it; file new material received at front of files
   C. put a temporary "out" folder in place of the one removed, giving title or subject, date removed, and who has it; put into this temporary folder any new material received
   D. keep a list of all folders removed and who has them; forward any new material received for filing while a folder is out to the person who has it

7._____

8. Folders labeled "Miscellaneous" should be used in an alphabetic filing system MAINLY to
   A. provide quick access to recent material
   B. avoid setting up individual folders for infrequent correspondence
   C. provide temporary storage for less important documents
   D. temporarily hold papers which will not fit into already crowded individual folders

8._____

9. Out-of-date and seldom-used records should be removed periodically from the files because
   A. overall responsibility for records will be transferred to the person in charge of the central storage files
   B. duplicate copies of every record are not needed
   C. valuable filing space will be regained and the time needed to find a current record will be cut down
   D. worthwhile suggestions on improving the filing system will result whenever this is done

9._____

10. Of the following, the BEST reason for discarding certain material from office files would be that the
    A. files are crowded
    B. material in the files is old
    C. material duplicates information obtainable from other sources in the files
    D. material is referred to most often by employees in an adjoining office

10._____

11. Of the following, the MAIN factor contributing to the expense of maintaining an office procedure manual would be the
    A. infrequent use of the manual
    B. need to revise it regularly
    C. cost of loose-leaf binders
    D. high cost of printing

    11.____

12. The suggestion that memos or directives which circulate among subordinates be initialed by each employee is a
    A. *poor* one, because, with modern copying machines, it would be possible to supply every subordinate with a copy of each message for his personal use
    B. *good* one, because it relieves the supervisor of blame for the action of subordinates who have read and initialed the messages
    C. *poor* one, because initialing the memo or directive is no guarantee that the subordinate has read the material
    D. *good* one, because it can be used as a record by the supervisor to show that his subordinates have received the message and were responsible for reading it

    12.____

13. Of the following, the MOST important reason for microfilming office records is to
    A. save storage space needed to keep records
    B. make it easier to get records when needed
    C. speed up the classification of information
    D. shorten the time which records must be kept

    13.____

14. Your office filing cabinets have become so overcrowded that it is difficult to use the files.
    Of the following, the MOST desirable step for you to take FIRST to relieve this situation would be to
    A. assign your assistant to spend some time each day reviewing the material in the files and to give you his recommendations as to what material may be discarded
    B. discard all material which has been in the files more than a given number of years
    C. submit a request for additional filing cabinets in your next budget request
    D. transfer enough material to the central storage room of your agency to give you the amount of additional filing space needed

    14.____

15. In indexing names of business firms and other organizations, one of the rules to be followed is:
    A. The word "and" is considered an indexing unit
    B. When a firm name includes the full name of a person who is not well known, the person's first name is considered as the first indexing unit
    C. Usually, the units in a firm name are indexed in the order in which they are written
    D. When a firm's name is made up of single letters (such as ABC Corp.), the letters taken together are considered as more than one indexing unit

    15.____

4 (#1)

16. Assume that your unit processes confidential forms which are submitted by persons seeking financial assistance. An individual comes to your office, gives you his name, and states that he would like to look over a form which he sent in about a week ago because he believes he omitted some important information.
Of the following, the BEST thing for you to do FIRST is to
    A. locate the proper form
    B. call the individual's home telephone number to verify his identity
    C. ask the individual if he has proof of his identity
    D. call the security office

17. An employee has been assigned to open her division head's mail and place it on his desk. One day, the employee opens a letter which she then notices is marked "Personal."
Of the following, the BEST action for her to take is to
    A. write "Personal" on the letter and staple the envelope to the back of the letter
    B. ignore the matter and treat the letter the same way as the others
    C. give it to another division head to hold until her own division head comes into the office
    D. leave the letter in the envelope and write "Sorry-opened by mistake" on the envelope, and initial it

18. The MOST important reason for having a filing system is to
    A. get papers out of the way
    B. have a record of everything that has happened
    C. retain information to justify your actions
    D. enable rapid retrieval of information

19. The system of filing which is used MOST frequently is called _____ filing.
    A. alphabetic   B. alphanumeric
    C. geographic   D. numeric

20. In judging the adequacy of a standard office form, which of the following is LEAST important?
    A. Date of the form   B. Legibility of the form
    C. Size of the form   D. Design of the form

21. Assume that the letters and reports which are dictated to you fall into a few distinct subject-matter areas.
The practice of trying to familiarize yourself with the terminology in these areas is
    A. *good*, because you will have a basis for commenting on the dictated material
    B. *good*, because it will be easier to take the dictation at the rate at which it is given
    C. *poor*, because the functions and policies of an office are not of your concern
    D. *poor*, because it will take too much time away from your assigned work

22. A letter was dictated on June 9 and was ready to be typed on June 12. The letter was typed on June 13, signed on June 14, and mailed on June 14. The date that, ORDINARILY, should have appeared on the letter is June
    A. 9   B. 12   C. 13   D. 14

    22.____

23. Of the following, the BEST reason for putting the "key point" at the beginning of a letter is that it
    A. may save time for the reader
    B. is standard practice in writing letters
    C. will more likely to be typed correctly
    D. cannot logically be placed elsewhere

    23.____

24. As a supervisor, you have been asked to attend committee meetings and take the minutes.
    The body of such minutes GENERALLY consists of
    A. the date and place of the meeting and the list of persons present
    B. an exact verbatim report of everything that was said by each person who spoke
    C. a clear description of each matter discussed and the action decided on
    D. the agenda of the meeting

    24.____

25. When typing a rough draft from a recorded transcription, a stenographer under your supervision reaches a spot on the recording that is virtually inaudible.
    Of the following, the MOST advisable action that you should recommend to her is to
    A. guess what the dictator intended to say based on what he said in the parts that are clear
    B. ask the dictator to listen to his unsatisfactory recording
    C. leave an appropriate amount of space for that portion that is inaudible
    D. stop typing the draft and send a note to the dictator identifying the item that could not be completed

    25.____

KEY (CORRECT ANSWERS)

1.	D	11.	B
2.	D	12.	D
3.	B	13.	A
4.	C	14.	A
5.	C	15.	C
6.	B	16.	C
7.	C	17.	D
8.	B	18.	D
9.	C	19.	A
10.	C	20.	A

21. B
22. D
23. A
24. C
25. C

TEST 2

DIRECTIONS: Each question or incomplete statement is followed by several suggested answers or completions. Select the one that BEST answers the question or completes the statement. *PRINT THE LETTER OF THE CORRECT ANSWER IN THE SPACE AT THE RIGHT.*

1. To tell a newly employed clerk to fill a top drawer of a four-drawer cabinet with heavy binders which will be often used and to keep lower drawers only partly filled is
   A. *good*, because a tall person would have to bend unnecessarily if he had to use a lower drawer
   B. *bad*, because the file cabinet may tip over when the top drawer is opened
   C. *good*, because it is the most easily reachable drawer for the average person
   D. *bad*, because a person bending down at another drawer may accidentally bang his head on the bottom of the drawer when he straightens up

   1.____

2. If you have requisitioned a "ream" of paper in order to duplicate a single page office announcement, how many announcements can be printed from the one package of paper?
   A. 200   B. 500   C. 700   D. 1,000

   2.____

3. In the operations of a government agency, a voucher is ORDINARILY used to
   A. refer someone to the agency for a position or assignment
   B. certify that an agency's records of financial transactions are accurate
   C. order payment from agency funds of a stated amount to an individual
   D. enter a statement of official opinion in the records of the agency

   3.____

4. Of the following types of cards used in filing systems, the one which is generally MOST helpful in locating records which might be filed under more than one subject is the _____ card.
   A. out
   B. tickler
   C. cross-reference
   D. visible index

   4.____

5. The type of filing system in which one does NOT need to refer to a card index in order to find the folder is called
   A. alphabetic   B. geographic   C. subject   D. locational

   5.____

6. Of the following, records management is LEAST concerned with
   A. the development of the best method for retrieving important information
   B. deciding what records should be kept
   C. deciding the number of appointments a client will need
   D. determining the types of folders to be used

   6.____

7. If records are continually removed from a set of files without "charging" them to the borrower, the filing system will soon become ineffective.
Of the following terms, the one which is NOT applied to a form used in the charge-out system is a
   A. requisition card
   B. out-folder
   C. record retrieval form
   D. substitution card

8. A new clerk has been told to put 500 cards in alphabetical order. Another clerk suggests that she divide the cards into four groups, such as A to F, G to L, M to R, and S to Z, and then alphabetize these four smaller groups.
The suggested method is
   A. *poor*, because the clerk will have to handle the sheets more than once and will waste time
   B. *good*, because it saves time, is more accurate, and is less tiring
   C. *good*, because she will not have to concentrate on it so much when it is in smaller groups
   D. *poor*, because this method is much more tiring than straight alphabetizing

9. In Microsoft Excel, data and records are entered into
   A. pages   B. forms   C. cells   D. contracts

10. Suppose a clerk has been given pads of pre-printed forms to use when taking phone messages for others in her office. The clerk is then observed using scraps of paper and not the forms for writing her messages.
It should be explained that the BEST reason for using the forms is that
   A. they act as a checklist to make sure that the important information is taken
   B. she is expected to do her work in the same way as others in the office
   C. they make sure that unassigned paper is not wasted on phone messages
   D. learning to use these forms will help train her to use more difficult forms

11. The high-speed printing process used for producing large quantities of superior quality copy and cost efficiency is called
   A. photocopying
   B. laser printing
   C. inkjet printing
   D. word processing

12. Of the following, the MAIN reason a stock clerk keeps a perpetual inventory of supplies in the storeroom is that such an inventory will
   A. eliminate the need for a physical inventory
   B. provide a continuous record of supplies on hand
   C. indicate whether a shipment of supplies is satisfactory
   D. dictate the terms of the purchase order

13. As a supervisor, you may be required to handle different types of correspondence.
    Of the following types of letters, it would be MOST important to promptly seal which kind of letter?
    A. One marked "confidential"
    B. Those containing enclosures
    C. Any letter to be sent airmail
    D. Those in which copies will be sent along with the original

14. While opening incoming mail, you notice that one letter indicates that an enclosure was to be included but, even after careful inspection, you are not able to find the information to which this refers.
    Of the following, the thing that you should do FIRST is
    A. replace the letter in its envelope and return it to the sender
    B. file the letter until the sender's office mails the missing information
    C. type out a letter to the sender informing him of his error
    D. make a notation in the margin of the letter that the enclosure was omitted

15. You have been given a checklist and assigned the responsibility of inspecting certain equipment in the various offices of your agency.
    Which of the following is the GREATEST advantage of the checklist?
    A. It indicates which equipment is in greatest demand.
    B. Each piece of equipment on the checklist will be checked only once.
    C. It helps to insure that the equipment listed will not be overlooked.
    D. The equipment listed suggests other equipment you should look for.

16. The BEST way to evaluate the overall state of completion of a construction project is to check the progress estimate against the
    A. inspection worksheet B. construction schedule
    C. inspector's checklist D. equipment maintenance schedule

17. The usual contract for agency work includes a section entitled "Instructions to Bidders," which states that the
    A. contractor agrees that he has made his own examination and will make no claim for damages on account of errors or omissions
    B. contractor shall not make claims for damages of any discrepancy, error, or omission in any plans
    C. estimates of quantities and calculations are guaranteed by the agency to be correct and are deemed to be a representation of the conditions affecting the work
    D. plans, measurements, dimensions, and conditions under which the work is to be performed are guaranteed by the agency

18. In order to avoid disputes over payments for extra work in a contract for construction, the BEST procedure to follow would be to
    A. have contractor submit work progress reports daily
    B. insert a special clause in the contract specifications
    C. have a representative on the job at all times to verify conditions
    D. allocate a certain percentage of the cost of the job to cover such expenses

19. Prior to the installation of equipment called for in the specifications, the contractor is USUALLY required to submit for approval 19.____
    A. sets of shop drawings
    B. a set of revised specifications
    C. a detailed description of the methods of work to be used
    D. a complete list of skilled and unskilled tradesmen he proposes to use

20. During the actual construction work, the CHIEF value of a construction schedule is to 20.____
    A. insure that the work will be done on time
    B. reveal whether production is falling behind
    C. show how much equipment and material is required for the project
    D. furnish data as to the methods and techniques of construction operations

KEY (CORRECT ANSWERS)

1.	B	11.	B
2.	B	12.	B
3.	C	13.	A
4.	C	14.	D
5.	A	15.	C
6.	C	16.	B
7.	C	17.	A
8.	B	18.	C
9.	C	19.	A
10.	A	20.	B

www.ingramcontent.com/pod-product-compliance
Lightning Source LLC
Chambersburg PA
CBHW081829300426
44116CB00014B/2522